Effective Communication for a Career in Law Enforcement

Susan Collins and Jan Olson

1999

EMOND MONTGOMERY PUBLICATIONS LIMITED

TORONTO, CANADA

Printed in Canada.

Edited, designed, and typeset by WordsWorth Communications, Toronto.
Cover design by Susan Darrach, Darrach Design.

Canadian Cataloguing in Publication Data

Collins, Susan, 1952–
    Effective communication for a career in law enforcement

(Police foundations program)
ISBN 1-55239-033-0

1. Communication in police administration.   2. Police reports — Authorship.
I. Olson, Jan, 1951–   . II. Title. III. Series.

HV7936.C79C64 1999   808'.066363   C99-930919-6

*For my friends and family for their
encouragement and support*
—Sue Collins

For my family, Brian, Kevin, and Matt
—Jan Olson

Contents

■ *Chapter 4*   ORAL PRESENTATIONS   75

■ *Chapter* 5   REPORT WRITING   135

Foreword

The purpose of this book is to present practical information for those individuals interested in undertaking a law enforcement career. The requirements in the broad area of communication are often overshadowed by the enforcement aspects of the job. The simple truth is that, to be successful in this career, you need good writing skills that reflect accuracy and contain relevant details, as well as strong persuasive and speaking abilities. Similarly, good listening skills, and the capacity to interpret non-verbal language, are occupational necessities in the unpredictable world of an officer.

These critical aspects of the law enforcement field are the focus of this book. The text is written in a manner similar to the writing style required by enforcement agencies: straightforward, factual, clear, and concise. Each chapter is accompanied by numerous exercises that allow the reader to practise what has been learned. The goal of the text is to create effective report writers, speakers, and communicators who are able to effectively function in a law enforcement environment.

CHAPTER 1
Listening

LISTENING CLUES

The ability to listen is one of the most important skills a law enforcement officer possesses. Daily, you may listen to other officers, superiors, complainants, victims, bystanders, suspects, informants, and law breakers, to name just a few. In almost every situation in which you find yourself, the ability to listen well allows you to complete your job more quickly and efficiently.

Listening is a communication process that involves both the speaker and the listener. Both participants constantly give feedback through verbal and non-verbal clues, whether they are communicating in person or over the telephone. In other words, each participant listens to both the other's voice and actions. There are also distractions that interfere with the participant's ability to communicate, and they must be overcome.

Speaker's Verbal Clues

The speaker's job is to present information so that the listener is able to understand and, in some instances, act on it. He or she also answers the listener's questions and reacts to the listener's non-verbal feedback. To do this, the speaker may speed up or slow down, speak more loudly or softly, repeat information, or put particular emphasis on words or points. The speaker also shows his or her interest in the information by putting enthusiasm or excitement in his or her voice.

Speaker's Non-Verbal Clues

To promote and retain the listener's interest, the speaker must appear interested in the information. Smiling, frowning, making or avoiding eye contact, slouching or standing/sitting stiffly, shaking a fist, and silence each send a message to the listener. Even if the speaker is really interested in a topic, his or her non-verbal clues can alienate the listener, which would be particularly detrimental in a courtroom, or when interviewing a victim or witness.

Listener's Verbal Clues

The listener's job is to assimilate the information, understand it, and, in some instances, act on it. If he or she is uncertain, the listener may ask the speaker to repeat information, or may ask questions or for examples. This uncertainty may stem from the speaker's contradictory verbal and non-verbal messages. For example, if the speaker expresses remorse for an action, but smiles and laughs while expressing this remorse, it may cause confusion for the listener, and clarification will be needed.

If the listener chats with a neighbour while the speaker is talking, this shows a disregard for the speaker and for what he or she is saying. It may prevent the listener from receiving all the necessary information because the speaker may simply stop talking.

Listener's Non-Verbal Clues

If the listener is silent, nods, smiles, or frowns; leans forward with interest or slouches; concentrates on the speaker or gazes away; or busies himself or herself with unrelated materials, a message is sent to the speaker. This may annoy the speaker or cause him or her to change his or her approach. However, the listener can never be sure which reaction it will promote, and he or she wouldn't want to alienate a witness who has necessary information.

Distractions

There are always things that interfere with listening. Even if the speaker and listener were locked in a small windowless room with no furnishings, there would still be deterrents to listening. Distractions include physiological, psychological, emotional, and semantic influences on the listener, as well as the physical environment where the communication occurs.

1. Physiological influences are those that occur when the listener is hungry, tired, cold, or uncomfortable.

2. Psychological influences are those that occur when the listener's mind is not on the topic, but on something else that is of greater importance to him or her.

3. Emotional influences are those that occur when the listener is upset, worried, angry, or excited.

4. Semantic influences are those that occur when the listener doesn't understand what the speaker is saying, possibly because of language or cultural barriers, or because the speaker uses words, phrases, or acronyms that the listener doesn't understand.

5. The physical environment may be too noisy or visually distracting for the listener to pay close attention to what the speaker is saying.

Whenever possible, it's important to try to overcome these distractions and focus on the speaker and what he or she is saying. By doing this the listener can get a clearer picture, and better understand the speaker's intended meaning.

■ **EXERCISE 1.1   LISTENING AND MEMORY**

E X E R C I S E

The teacher has recorded a brief message on a piece of flip-chart paper and has taped that paper upside down on the chalkboard so that it cannot be read.

1. Six students participate as subjects and number themselves from one to six; a seventh student (student 7) assists the teacher. The remaining students in the class act as observers.

2. Subjects 2 to 6 leave the room while the brief pre-printed message is read to subject 1 by student 7. The audience does not hear the message relayed to subject 1.

3. Subject 1 attempts to retain as much of the message as possible. Subject 2 is brought into the classroom and subject 1 repeats the message out loud as accurately as possible to subject 2.

4. Once subject 1 has completed the communication to subject 2, he or she sits down and remains silent. The class will also be silent throughout the exercise.

5. Subject 3 is now brought into the room and subject 2 relays the message to subject 3. Then subject 2 sits down and remains silent throughout the rest of the exercise.

6. The pattern continues, with subject 3 transmitting the message to subject 4, subject 4 to subject 5, and subject 5 to subject 6.

7. Subject 6 speaks the final message, clearly, out loud. Student 7, who first read the message to subject 1, records subject 6's words on the chalkboard.

8. The seventh student removes the printed message from the chalkboard and flips it over so that the class can see the original message.

The two messages are compared. The following questions may now be answered:

1. What is the difference, if any?

2. What was omitted? Why do you think these particular parts of the message were missed?

(Exercise 1.1 is continued on the next page.)

(Exercise 1.1 continued ...)

3. What was distorted? Why?

4. What have you learned from this exercise: as a speaker, and as a listener?

5. What suggestions would you give to a speaker and a listener as a result of this exercise?

LISTENING ACTIVELY

As illustrated in the previous exercise, listening is not simply hearing. It requires active involvement between speaker and listener. This enables you, the listener, to understand, empathize with, and react to what is said. In order to listen well, you must actively participate with the speaker:

1. Ask questions for clarification.

2. Ask for examples to help you better understand.

3. Pay attention to what is said. Don't busy yourself trying to develop good questions to ask.

4. Focus on the speaker to show your interest. Look at the speaker. If you're sitting, lean forward in your chair; if you're standing, stand up straight.

5. Use non-verbal cues to show that you're paying attention. This encourages the speaker to continue, and gives him or her a sense of security.

6. Concentrate on the message or information presented. Don't allow your mind to wander onto unrelated issues, and don't let outside influences such as the temperature or your own emotional or physical condition distract you.

7. Note both verbal and non-verbal messages. Look for agreement and contradictions in speech and body language. (See chapter 3 on non-verbal communication for more details.)

8. Listen to what is said from the speaker's point of view. (In other words, put yourself in the speaker's position.) This use of empathy enables you to better understand

   a. what he or she is saying,

   b. the reasons behind what he or she is saying, and

   c. the underlying emotions that may be affecting what he or she is saying.

9. Control your own emotions so that you can react appropriately and with confidence.

Having to ask someone to repeat previously stated information can be embarrassing, and it demonstrates your lack of professionalism. By listening actively, you can better understand the information presented, relate to the speaker, and respond appropriately.

EXERCISE

■ **EXERCISE 1.2   OBSERVATION AND MEMORY**

1. A videotape depicting a controversial subject is shown to the class. During the video the students have their workbooks closed and they carefully watch the video without taking notes.

2. The teacher asks a series of questions concerning the content of the video in order to test observation skills and memory retention:

   a. What different points of view are shown in this video?

   b. Which point of view do you personally hold?

   c. From which point of view was more information presented?

   d. How much information did you notice that did not agree with your point of view?

   e. What have you learned from this exercise?

CHAPTER 2
The Writing Process

KNOWING YOUR AUDIENCE AND PURPOSE

As a law enforcement officer, you may be asked to prepare information for, or report on, many different groups of people. The people you come in contact with in your profession will probably have more varied backgrounds than those others would meet in any other profession. You may be asked to communicate with the business community, city council, special interest groups, parents, students of all ages, senior citizens, fellow officers and your superiors, and many others. You must, therefore, be prepared to relate to each of these groups, taking their interests, their well-being and the well-being of others, and the law into consideration. One of your most important tasks is to get your message across without sounding condescending, superior, or unfeeling.

In many instances, the purpose of your presentations, whether they be written or oral, will be similar for different audiences, but they'll have a different slant because of the age, maturity, interests, and background of your audience. For example, suppose you are asked to prepare information about Block Parents for a local community group, and also for a group of kindergarten children. Your purpose may be child safety in both cases. For the adults, however, your slant may be the importance of protecting their children and providing a safe environment for them to grow up in. For the children, your slant may be that there are places they can go where they will be safe if they feel uneasy or threatened, and that there are people in the community looking out for them.

Obviously, your presentation styles will vary according to your audience. You wouldn't present the Block Parent information to the kindergarten children and community group in the same way. It's important that you take the time to understand the needs and, in this instance, the attention span of your audience into account. The adults need to know that there is something they can do to help make their community safe. Usually, adults need less repetition than children; however, they may not accept information at face value. You may need to justify your information by offering proof, or appeal to their emotions to encourage them to act. The children need to know that their community is a safe place to grow up. Their attention span is often much shorter than that of adults, and they don't need to know all the details the adults may be given. Different activities to reinforce the information will help instill it in the children's minds.

The following sample program on bicycle safety shows how you as a police officer must consider both the purpose of your information and the importance of knowing the audience you are addressing.

Sample Program: Bicycle Safety

Suppose you're asked to write a program for, or speak about, bicycle safety to two groups of people. One is a group of grade 3 and 4 students, and the other is a group of parents at a home and school meeting. Obviously, your audiences are different, so your approach will be different for each group.

Purpose

Before you begin, you must establish your purpose (what it is you want your audience to do) after learning about bicycle safety. Although the purposes for the two groups are similar, they must have a different slant. For the children, your purpose is to get them to wear their equipment properly and ride safely on the streets. For the adults, your purpose is to make them aware that accidents are frequently serious, and that they should make sure their children have helmets, wear them properly, and obey the traffic laws.

Children

For the students in grades 3 and 4, you may plan an hour's presentation on bicycle safety. This shouldn't simply be a lecture, because the students will probably lose interest within the first few minutes. It will need to involve about five steps:

1. Ask questions to discover what the children already know. You will elicit many responses when you ask such things as:

    a. Who owns a bicycle helmet?

    b. Who wears their helmet every time they ride their bike?

    c. Who makes sure their helmet is fastened properly?

    d. Who knows the hand signals for turns?

    e. Who signals their turns?

    f. Are there traffic rules you should obey when you're riding your bike?

    g. How should you cross an intersection when you're on your bike?

2. Supply information that's not too sophisticated or frightening. Let them know that they can be hurt if they don't obey the rules, but don't scare them. Inform them of such things as

    a. how important it is that they don't wear their helmets backward,

    b. how to make sure their helmets fit properly and why,

    c. what signals to use when they turn,

    d. they must stop at stop signs and red stoplights, and

    e. how to safely cross at an intersection.

3. Demonstrate as much of the information as you can, and get the children to participate. The more participation you elicit, the better their attention and understanding will be. Mix the demonstrations with the information:

    a. When you discuss wearing helmets the right way, show them how easy it is to knock a backward helmet off someone's forehead.

    b. When you discuss helmets fitting properly, show them how to tighten their chin straps, and have the children fit their helmets on themselves and each other.

    c. When you discuss signalling turns, have the children practise with you.

4. Play games to encourage everyone to participate, and to reinforce what you've said:

    a. Put the helmets in a pile, and have a race to see how many can find their own helmet and put it on properly.

    b. Play a game such as Simon Says to practise hand signals for turns.

    c. Divide the children into teams and have them put their helmets on properly and either ride or walk a course using the correct hand signals.

5. Quiz the children briefly at the end to make sure that they understand what you have discussed and practised. This also allows you the opportunity to answer any questions they may have.

Adults

For the parents at a home and school meeting, you need to spend far less time on bicycle safety. You could effectively present your information in 10 to 15 minutes. Although you wouldn't use the same methods that you used with the children because of the adults' maturity and level of understanding, your presentation must still involve about four steps:

1. Discuss the need for bicycle safety, to make the adults more aware of its importance:

    a. Present accident statistics.

    b. Show pictures of children in bicycle accidents.

    c. Describe scenes of children cycling into and in traffic.

    d. Explain the consequences of some bicycle accidents.

2. Supply information to the adults so that they are more aware of how they can help prevent bicycle accidents:

    a. Stress the safety aspects of insisting their children wear a helmet.

    b. Explain the importance of properly fitting their children's helmets.

    c. Discuss the importance of hand signals for turns.

    d. Explain the need for children to obey stop signs and stoplights.

    e. Explain the proper procedures for crossing at an intersection.

3. Demonstrate such things as:

    a. how to determine the proper helmet sizes for children,

    b. how to properly fit children's helmets, and

    c. the proper hand signals that are used for turns.

4. Review the need for bicycle safety training for children and the adults' role in helping to prevent injury. You may have some adults practise fitting a helmet.

EXERCISE

■ EXERCISE 2.1   UNDERSTANDING YOUR AUDIENCE AND PURPOSE

Choose one of the situations and audiences below, and do the following:

1. Explain the purpose of your report or presentation for each audience.

2. Explain the slant of your report or presentation for each audience.

3. Detail the information you would present to each audience.

Situations	Audiences
1. Teenagers' use of non-prescription drugs	Teenagers and parents
2. Bullying at school	10- to 12-year-olds and parents

(Exercise 2.1 is continued on the next page.)

(Exercise 2.1 continued ...)

3. Sexual harassment in the workplace	Men and women
4. Mandatory gun licensing	Hunters and anti-gun lobbyists
5. Young drivers drinking and driving	17- to 19-year-olds and city council
6. Eleven p.m. noise curfew	Party-goers and upset neighbours
7. Personal safety	5- and 6-year-olds and senior citizens

WRITING AN ESSAY

There are three main types of essays. There are those written to persuade (persuasive essays), those to explain (expository essays), and those to simply share information or experiences (descriptive and narrative essays). In a report, the details of the offence section requires the use of the narrative essay writing technique. A research essay uses either expository or persuasive essay writing techniques. No matter which type of essay you write, it's important that you know your audience and purpose first. Once you have established these, collecting information and writing the actual essay is less difficult because you have a direction.

Collecting Information

Collecting information for your essay may prove to be the most demanding yet interesting part of the whole writing process. This is when you get to throw ideas around and find out how others feel about your topic. In fact, you may even be persuaded to change your mind about some subjects. It takes time to do a thorough job, so allow yourself plenty of time to collect your information before you have to write. There are five parts to collecting information: brainstorming, eliminating unnecessary material, organizing information, researching information, and documenting your sources.

1. Brainstorming

The first step in collecting information is brainstorming. This involves writing down your purpose and then recording anything that relates to it, even if you don't agree with the point. At this time, don't worry about whether or not you can use all the information you record. Just make sure that you don't leave out anything that may be important or of interest.

2. Eliminating Unnecessary Information

Once you have written your brainstorming list, go through it and eliminate any information that does not pertain directly to the main idea of your essay. You may find some things that are interesting, but if they don't support your purpose, now's the time to get rid of them. This step is necessary because it ensures that you don't waste valuable time on unimportant or unrelated details.

3. Organizing Your Information

You need to organize the information that is left on your brainstorming list, so you know which pieces fit together, and you have some direction to your research. It's helpful if you make an outline indicating the main points you'll discuss and their supporting ideas. This adds order to your information, and it's something to which you can refer as you do your research, to make sure you stay on topic.

4. Researching Information

You may need to research information to supply depth to your paper. Facts, details, and examples can all be used to support your main idea. You may find them by observing, interviewing, searching the Internet or a CD-ROM, or looking in books or periodicals in the library, among other things. Don't limit your research to one source, and make sure that the sources you choose are reliable. Also, check to ensure that the information you gather is relevant to your purpose.

5. Documenting Your Sources

Make a note of every source you consult. This note includes the name of the source, the volume or edition, the author(s), the publisher, the date and place of publication, and the page numbers you used or read. This information must later be recorded at the end of your essay.

Drafting the Essay

Essays are ordered in different ways, depending on your objectives. The most common order used in law enforcement writing is chronological. When you write chronologically, the information in your paper flows logically from the past to the present. Another order used by law enforcement officers is spatial. This is a method of describing spaces such as house interiors and exteriors, and other areas under investigation. Other ways that essays are ordered include cause and effect, order of importance, familiar to unfamiliar, and comparison and contrast. No matter how your essay is ordered, it must contain three important parts: an introduction, a body, and a conclusion. The text of your essay should be carefully edited to make sure that it is free of errors, so that your reader can concentrate on the content without being distracted by careless errors. Besides an introduction, body, and conclusion, you will probably also need a title page and documentation.

1. Introduction

The first paragraph (or two) of the essay is the introduction. It contains the purpose of your essay, which is also referred to as the thesis statement or topic. It also indicates the slant of your essay. Usually the introduction is just a few sentences, but it indicates the order in which information will be discussed. This paragraph is also used to attract your reader's interest and attention.

Expect that you will make some changes to your first version of the introduction. It is there to give your initial draft some direction. However, after you finish writing the body of your essay, you may realize you have changed the slant or altered the main idea and so must alter the introduction to accommodate this change.

2. Body

Following the introduction is the body or discussion of your essay. Depending on the breadth of your topic, this section may be one or two paragraphs, or it may stretch for pages. Here you discuss the main idea in depth and in detail, following the order indicated in the introduction. This section may include observations, interview information, or research material you have gathered from other sources. It may also include your own ideas supported by research you have done. Remember that for any quoted or paraphrased information, you must identify the source(s) using the endnote method, as explained in the documentation section of this chapter, below.

3. Conclusion

The essay must close with a conclusion. Here you may summarize what you have discussed, or draw conclusions, or make recommendations based on the facts presented in the discussion. The conclusion should contain no new ideas! It simply ends your essay.

Editing

Once you have written your first draft, don't think you are finished. A well-written essay may take five or six revisions to get the information to flow smoothly. Be sure to edit your ideas carefully to make sure that everything you discuss relates to your purpose. Make sure that your information is presented logically and clearly, so that your reader has no difficulty understanding your paper. Correct any grammar or spelling errors that detract from your purpose. Your final draft should be polished and professionally presented (keyed if written out of class). See the sample edit sheet that follows this section. It can be used after each draft of your essay and again before you hand your essay in for grading.

Works Cited

At the end of your essay, on a separate sheet of paper, is the works cited section. Here you list your sources in the manner described in the documentation section of this chapter.

Title Page

Finally, before submitting your essay for grading, create a title page. This page clearly states the title of your essay in the middle of the page. It also lists the following: your name, student number, class number, course name, instructor's name, and the essay due date. This information is found on the last six lines, in the bottom right corner of the page. Don't forget to staple your essay together before submitting it for grading!

Essay Edit Sheet

The following sample edit sheet may be used after each draft of your essay. There may be a few things in this checklist that don't apply to your essay, so ignore them. There may also be problems you have experienced that aren't addressed in this checklist, so make a note of them and watch out for them in your own essay. You may use this sheet to edit your own essay, or have someone else read it to check for the things listed.

Content

For your essay to be free of errors, you should be able to answer "Yes" to each of the points listed below.

Introduction:	Yes _____	No _____	Contains purpose/thesis statement
	Yes _____	No _____	Indicates slant of the essay
	Yes _____	No _____	Indicates order of discussion of information
	Yes _____	No _____	Attracts interest/attention of the reader

Body:	Yes _____	No _____	Clearly follows order stated in introduction
	Yes _____	No _____	Each point addresses the main idea
	Yes _____	No _____	Each new idea is in a new paragraph
	Yes _____	No _____	Contains supporting details/examples
	Yes _____	No _____	Details/examples clearly apply to main ideas
	Yes _____	No _____	Facts are clearly presented
	Yes _____	No _____	Inferences are identified as such
	Yes _____	No _____	Information is current and relevant
	Yes _____	No _____	Depth of research is apparent
	Yes _____	No _____	Quoted/paraphrased material is endnoted
Conclusion:	Yes _____	No _____	Summarizes information discussed
	Yes _____	No _____	Draws conclusions based on body
	Yes _____	No _____	Makes recommendations based on body
	Yes _____	No _____	Contains no new ideas

Style

For your essay to be free of errors, you should be able to answer "No" to each of the points listed below.

Grammar:	Yes _____	No _____	Fragment sentences
	Yes _____	No _____	Run-on sentences
	Yes _____	No _____	Comma errors
	Yes _____	No _____	Apostrophe errors
	Yes _____	No _____	Parallelism errors
	Yes _____	No _____	Wordiness errors
Spelling:	Yes _____	No _____	Words misspelled
	Yes _____	No _____	Homonyms used (see Writing Pitfalls, page 217)
	Yes _____	No _____	Incorrect words for intended meaning

Documentation and Appearance

Don't concern yourself with this section until you have completed the final version of your essay. Only then is it necessary to consult the checklist below.

For your essay to be free of errors, you should be able to answer "Yes" to each of the points listed below.

Works cited:	Yes _____	No _____	Follows documentation guidelines
	Yes _____	No _____	Grammar/spelling error-free
	Yes _____	No _____	On a separate page
Title page:	Yes _____	No _____	Title of essay
	Yes _____	No _____	Title in centre of page
	Yes _____	No _____	Identification information in bottom right corner
	Yes _____	No _____	Grammar/spelling error free
	Yes _____	No _____	On a separate page
Overall:	Yes _____	No _____	Information is logically presented
	Yes _____	No _____	Information flows smoothly
	Yes _____	No _____	Essay is neatly typed
	Yes _____	No _____	Typing is double-spaced
	Yes _____	No _____	Essay is stapled

DOCUMENTATION

Documentation allows the reader of your essay to locate the material used during research, thus allowing him or her to check its accuracy, to read the original work, or to learn further details. The two most commonly used styles or methods are:

1. endnotes and references or works cited, and

2. footnotes and bibliography.

Endnote Method

The endnote method is the more modern method of the two and is easier to use. It has the following features:

1. Parentheses surround information that identifies what source was used in that particular part of the essay. For example:

> When questioned about the crime rate, many Canadians will say that it is on the rise. Contrary to this popular belief, the crime rate has been decreasing over the past five years. Likewise, incidents of violent crime have dropped (Singh 154). To what factors can we attribute this decrease in crime? The purpose of this presentation is to inform you about these factors.

"(Singh 154)" tells the reader that the information concerning a drop in violent crime is located on page 154 of a source written by someone with the last name Singh. The reader cannot tell if Singh wrote a book or an article. The works cited at the end of the essay will divulge this information.

2. A works cited section is placed on the last page(s) of the essay. The works cited are listed in alphabetical order according to the author's last name, or by the title of the source if no author is given. The works cited are not numbered. For example:

> Singh, E. *Crime Rates and What They Tell.* Toronto: Pica Publications, 1998.

The parenthetical reference in the body—containing the author's last name and page number or numbers ("(Singh 154)")—supplies the reader with enough information to identify the corresponding author or source in the list of works cited at the end of the essay. The works cited section lists all sources from which ideas, quotations, and information were obtained. Whenever the reader sees Singh noted in the essay, he or she knows that full details of the information source will be located at the end of the essay, in the works cited section. All the reader has to do is refer to the alphabetical list of authors and locate the full information from Singh's book *Crime Rates and What They Tell.*

The List of Works Cited

The works cited section is located at the end of the essay on a separate page. The works cited page(s) should be numbered in sequence with the pages of the essay. For example, if the text of your essay ended on page 8, then the works cited would follow on page 9. The first line of each entry is at the left margin, with the lines that follow indented five spaces. Double space between entries.

Examples of Works Cited

Books

One Author

Forcese, Dennis P. *Policing Canadian Society.* Scarborough, ON: Prentice-Hall, 1992.

Note that the province is given only with lesser-known cities such as Scarborough or Guelph, not with well-known cities such as Toronto or Vancouver. In the body of the essay, the only information recorded concerning the reference to this source would be the author's last name and the page number where the information was discovered: "(Forcese 33)." The author's last name and the page number tell the reader that the piece of information just mentioned in the essay came from page 33 of Dennis Forcese's book *Policing Canadian Society.*

Two or Three Authors

Mewett, Alan W., and Morris Manning. *Mewett & Manning on Criminal Law.* Toronto: Butterworths, 1994.

Note that the first author's name is given surname first in order to follow the alphabetical order format. All other names occur in their normal order—that is, the first name, possibly second name or initial, followed by the surname.

Also note the five-space indentation of the second line and on. "(Mewett and Manning 16)" would be written in the body if information from page 16 of the above book were used.

More Than Three Authors

Heilbroner, Robert L., et al. *In the Name of Profit.* New York: Doubleday, 1992.

What would be written in the body of the essay if information from page 165 of the above book were used?

An Edition Other Than the First Edition

> Gibaldi, Joseph, and Walter S. Achtert. *MLA Handbook for Writers of Research Papers*. 2nd ed. New York: Modern Language Association, 1984.

One Part of Book by a Single Author

A part of a book might be an essay, article, or chapter:

> Ingham, Rory, M. "Death by Lethal Injection." *Capital Punishment: Arguments of the '90s*. Toronto: Pica Publications, 1998.

A Government Document

> Ontario Legislative Assembly. Standing Committee on Social Development. *Debates*. 3rd Session, 32nd Parliament. Toronto, 1993.

Entries for Articles in Periodicals

> Dosman, Edgar J. "Hemispheric Relations in the 1980's: A Perspective from Canada." *Journal of Canadian Studies* 19 (1984): 42-60.

Note the volume number "19." Volume 19, issue 4 would be written as "19.4."

A Magazine Article

> Kimber, Stephen. "Arrested Development." *Elm Street*. Oct. 1998: 31.

Note that all months except May, June, and July are abbreviated. What would be written in the body of your essay?

An Article from a Daily Newspaper

> Milner, Brian. "GATT Decries Growing Wave of Protectionism." *The Globe and Mail* [Toronto] 28 Mar. 1997, Metro ed.: B3.

Note the square brackets for the place of publication. What would be written in the body of your essay?

Not all newspaper articles have a byline (or author). Such articles would be documented like this:

"GATT Decries Growing Wave of Protectionism." *The Globe and Mail* [Toronto] 28 Mar. 1997, Metro ed.: B3.

This would be written in the body of your essay: "(*The Globe and Mail*, Mar. 28, 1997, B3)." Note that *The Globe and Mail* is keyed in italics.

Films and Videos

Powwow at Duck Lake. Prod. John Kemeny and Barrie Howells. Dir. Bonnie Klein. National Film Board of Canada, 1988.

Personal Communication

Clark, Merill P. Personal interview. 22 May 1998.

Identify the means of communication—for example, personal interview, telephone interview, letter, or e-mail.

CD-ROMs

Information used in an essay obtained from CD-ROM must be documented, like all resources used. In the works cited section, CD-ROM material would be documented like this:

Shamir, Edward. "Investigating Crime in Canada." *Maclean's*, 6 Dec. 1995, 87. Publisher (if there is any), Canadian Magazine Index.

What would be written in the body of your essay?

The Internet

The Internet has become a popular, quick method of obtaining information. Ensure that you are visiting a reputable site. By accessing Mohawk College's library home page, for example, you can obtain information from sites that have been updated in the past six months, and you can rely on the fact that the information is valid. Be warned that approximately 50 percent of the information on the Internet is junk! Following is a works cited example of a source from the Internet: RCMP's CAPRA training site:

"RCMP Learning and Development." http://www.RCMP-learning.org/capra.html (20 Jul. 1998).

Note that the date "(20 Jul. 1998)" indicates when you visited the site. What would be written in the body of your essay?

Using the Parenthetical Reference in the Essay (Endnotes): Highlights and Review

Use a parenthetical reference to draw an idea, piece of information, or quotation from a source collected during the research phase of your essay. The author's last name and the page number of the work are given in parentheses immediately following the borrowed information. The parenthetical reference is usually positioned at the end of a sentence. For example:

> Perhaps crime can be described as an act that offends the morals of the society (MacIntosh 20).

Note that the final punctuation (the period) is placed after the parenthesis. The above example is paraphrased from page 20 of a law book entitled *Fundamentals of the Criminal Justice System*. On the works cited page at the end of the essay, the reader can determine that the endnote refers to:

> MacIntosh, Donald A. *Fundamentals of the Criminal Justice System*. Toronto: Carswell, 1989.

If this example were a quotation, the parenthetical reference would occur after the quotation marks, but before the final punctuation mark. For example:

> "Perhaps crime ... of the society" (MacIntosh 20).

What if you are using two or more sources from the same author? Include a shortened version of the title of the reference with a comma separating the author's name and title—for example, "(MacIntosh, *Fundamentals* 117)."

Quotations

If the quotation is over four lines, then you place it in this format: single-spaced and indented from both left and right margins. At the conclusion of the quotation, place the final punctuation and then write the parenthetical reference as follows: "(Collins and Olson 21)."

Note that in the previous examples there is no mention of the word "page"; the author's name and page number are separated only by a single space. However, some other reference styles use the letter "p." for "page," or "pp." for "pages." Following are a few more examples:

◆ Citing works by more than one author—for example, "(Languor and Zasloff 5)."

◆ Citing information other than page numbers—for example, "(Ritter 3: 12)." The "3" stands for the volume number.

◆ If the reference information is mentioned in the sentence, do not repeat it in the endnote; simply record the page. For example:

> MacIntosh points out that 90 percent of all challenges under the *Charter of Rights and Freedoms* have been based on the sections pertaining to legal rights (27).

WRITING A SUMMARY

A summary, sometimes referred to as a précis or paraphrase, is a condensed version of an original article or text. It's written to present the main ideas of the original, while it eliminates unnecessary information. Often summaries are written not just to record information for your own purposes, but so that others can learn the content of the original without having to read the whole thing.

Information About Summaries

They should

1. be one-third of the original's length,

2. contain the main ideas of the original,

3. contain some but not necessarily all of the examples given in the original,

4. be written in your own words,

5. follow the order in which information is presented in the original,

6. reflect the weighting of information in the original,

7. reflect the slant or bias of the original,

8. not repeat information,

9. not simply join together quotes or passages from the original, and

10. not contain new information or your own ideas.

Most of us don't write summaries often enough to become proficient. Therefore, there are some rules you can follow to ensure that what you write actually is a summary and not just what you think the article says.

Rules for Summary Writing

1. Read the entire article from start to finish without stopping. This allows you to get a general understanding of the topic. Ignore words that you aren't familiar with, or else try to understand them from the context of the article.

2. Reread the article, and identify and look up the meanings of unfamiliar words, phrases, or terms. This will not only give you a better understanding of the original, but will also allow you to pick up anything you may have missed on your first reading.

3. Again read the original, and highlight or underline the main ideas. Often these are found in the first or last sentences of each paragraph, but this isn't always the case. Also highlight or underline important details such as terms, definitions, and examples. By doing this, you eliminate unnecessary or distracting information.

4. Then, without looking at the original, record what you remember from the original article. Ignoring the original may help you avoid plagiarism. Don't worry if you can't remember everything, just write down what you do remember.

5. Refer to the original to check what you have recorded. Make sure you haven't omitted main ideas or important details. Record what you have missed, but don't copy word for word from the original.

6. Make sure you haven't quoted passages from the original. If you have, rewrite the ideas in your own words. Remember that three or more words copied directly from the original constitutes plagiarism.

7. Write your summary from your notes.

8. Make sure you haven't repeated anything or added information that wasn't in the original article. If you have, eliminate it.

9. Make sure you haven't changed any information or added your own ideas. Everything you present should be from the original and should not reflect your own interpretation.

10. Make sure you haven't changed the bias or slant of the original. If the article presents a favourable side to something you oppose, ignore your own feelings or beliefs and present only what is in the article.

11. Count every word to make sure your summary is one-third the length of the original. If it is too short, you may need to return to the original for more information. If it is too long, eliminate information to make it the correct length. You may also rephrase information if your summary is just a little too long. For example, to eliminate five words, the statement:

> The officers arrested a person who was suspected of stealing the purse of the victim.

could be shortened to

> The officers arrested a suspect for stealing the victim's purse.

12. Give your summary a title that reflects the content but that is not the same as that of the original.

13. Finally, read your summary over carefully and check it for accuracy and for spelling and grammar errors.

Sample Article

The article "Listening Is Part of Communication," written by Barry Chodirker and taken from *Canadian Secretary*, May 1987, is reproduced below. The article is 811 words in length, so a summary of it should be between 260 and 280 words. Following the article is a sample summary. Notice how the summary is written in the writer's own words, but still reflects the main ideas and details of the original. Also, note that important terms are defined for the reader.

Listening Is Part of Communication

Good listening remains a fine art and rarer than one might imagine. Most of us spend about 70 percent of our day communicating (or trying!), and almost half of that figure involves listening. Nevertheless, listening is probably our least efficient communication skill. Generally, we don't do it well. Even as we might be trying to improve our writing, reading, and speaking, we oddly enough neglect the skill we use and need the most.

There are reasons, of course. Part of it is social, or cultural. Our society places a much higher premium on talking. It doesn't have to be meaningful or significant talk. It can be mindless drivel, but we prefer it to silence. We're uncomfortable with silence. We don't particularly trust it. We want to fill it.

When people around us aren't talking, we think something is wrong. We ask if they're not feeling well, or if something is troubling them. It's not that we are all that anxious to listen, either. We simply want them to talk.

If we're all busy talking, there's not much listening going on. There is a lot of fake listening masquerading as the real thing. We are all guilty of it, and we usually give ourselves away. We nod a lot, apparently signalling both attentiveness and understanding. It's likely a sham. The nodding is probably insincere, a substitute for paying attention.

It's not easy to be a good listener. It requires, strangely enough, a healthy regard for silence, particularly your own! What many of us don't realize is that it is a skill, developed through effort, perhaps even formal study. It's an active process, not a passive one. We confuse mere hearing, which involves no work at all, with listening, which can require a great deal of work. Those who do listen well aren't born with the skill. They work at it.

There are legitimate obstacles to overcome. The first, as we have noted, is your own tendency to talk. You might also have to fight your own impatience. Listening takes time, and you need to give it. Much of the fake listening I mentioned earlier involves an unwillingness to spend the time. If you're in a hurry to get away, the ever present nodding will invariably be accompanied by furtive glances at your watch!

Most of us are guilty as well of what experts call selective screening. As we listen, we filter things out, either by evaluating or judging what is coming in, or by translating it into something acceptable. In short, we often hear only what we want to hear. We all know how exasperating it can be to deal with someone who listens in that manner.

As if the other factors were not enough, there are usually some basic distractions at work as well. You are angry, worried, upset, hungry, too cold, too warm, too tired. There is always something to make it harder to listen. Is it any wonder that complimenting someone on being a good listener remains one of the most special accolades we can bestow?

Good speakers realize that most people simply are not good listeners, and so anticipate that reality when giving presentations. It is no accident that accomplished business and professional speakers rely heavily on visual aids when they are speaking to small groups. The strategic use of these aids actually promotes better listening.

We know that people learn as readily through the eyes (i.e., visually) as they do through the ears (i.e., verbally). Furthermore, visual aids help to focus the listener's attention. By skillfully weaving these devices into a presentation, the speaker is able to orchestrate that attention, thereby increasing the attention span. Drawings, charts, overheads, photographs, slides, and graphics of every description aren't there just for decoration.

There is a principle at work here called "chunking." It involves giving things to people in smaller rather than larger chunks. Visual aids complement this principle by reducing or softening lengthy, purely verbal descriptions. In other words, too much straight verbal without the balancing and shifting effect of the visual starts to discourage close listening. Using visual aids well requires skill, the kind that comes with practice. Too many aids can clutter a presentation. Any device used improperly or unnecessarily becomes a distraction. Be sure that what you use is pertinent, reinforces what you are saying, and where appropriate meets professional standards for scale and accuracy. Whenever you use props of any kind, it is perhaps wise to maintain a healthy respect for Murphy's Law, that whatever can go wrong probably will.

Finally, you don't need to be particularly fancy or ornate in your use of visual aids. A simple chalkboard might be all you require. The wonderful advantage of writing on the board is that it combines the visual with the verbal, promoting both kinds of learning simultaneously. That in itself commands attention from your audience.

Sample Summary

The summary of "Listening Is Part of Communication" is as follows.

Listening and Communicating

Good listening is a rare art. It is a communication skill we neglect even though it is important. Our society encourages people to talk. Even if it is insignificant, talking fills the uncomfortable void of silence.

We are all guilty of fake listening when we only pretend to listen. We may nod to indicate our attention and understanding, but it is likely insincere.

Being a good listener requires effort. It is an active process unlike mere hearing, which is passive. To become good listeners, we must overcome such obstacles as our own desire to talk and our impatience, and remember that listening takes time. Selective screening is a trap into which many of us fall. We filter things out by evaluating or translating what we hear, so we only hear what we want to hear.

Basic distractions such as being worried, hungry, cold, and tired also make it hard to listen. Good speakers know most of us don't listen well. Therefore, they use visual aids to encourage better listening. Such aids help focus our attention and increase our attention span. They reduce long verbal descriptions and allow the speaker to give us information in small bits. This process, called *chunking*, encourages listening.

Practise to use visual aids skillfully. Too many visuals and improperly used devices are ineffective. Visual aids should relate to and reinforce the topic, and should adhere to professional standards. Also, remember Murphy's Law.

Visual aids needn't be fancy. A visual aid as simple as a chalkboard combines verbal and visual learning and attracts the audience's attention.

The original is 811 words. The above summary is 262 words—about two-thirds listening, and one-third speaking—to reflect the weighting of the original.

PARAPHRASING EXERCISES

■ **EXERCISE 2.2   PARAPHRASING AN ARTICLE**

EXERCISE

To prepare for this exercise, read the following article on plagiarism.

Plagiarism

Plagiarism occurs if you use someone else's words, thoughts, theories, ideas, or research and claim them as your own. This breaks copyright laws. Besides being illegal, it is regarded, according to college policy, as "academic dishonesty," a fancy term for cheating. Even a short phrase copied directly is plagiarism, unless the words are placed in quotation marks and credit is given to the source. If you change only some of the words from another person's work, you are plagiarizing. Likewise, using someone else's argument, organization, style, and major points is also plagiarizing.

Any research paper will, of course, use facts, statistics, and ideas discovered from different sources. There is nothing wrong with using thoughts in this way, provided that you indicate the source and recognize the author from whom you learned the information. The original author's work is either:

1. quoted directly, word for word, as it appears in the source, or

2. it is paraphrased.

Paraphrasing means expressing an original idea in your own words. Because the idea belongs to someone else, it must be documented as an endnote. After you have paraphrased, check what you have written with the original version to ensure that you have not changed the intended meaning. Commonly known facts or ideas do not have to be acknowledged. For example: The new gun law makes it tougher to own a gun. Any essay or research usually consists of three things:

1. your opinion;

2. commonly known facts; and

3. information, research, graphs, tapes, computer information, books, newspaper articles, magazine articles, interviews, pamphlets, and the like.

Information that you did not know before you commenced the project, but learned from a source, must be endnoted. If you didn't know it before, then you learned it from someone else. That person receives credit for that information in the form of an endnote.

1. Paraphrase the content of the preceding article by rewriting the information in your own words. Hint: Eliminate any repetition.

(Exercise 2.2 is continued on the next page.)

(Exercise 2.2 continued ...)

2. Do not use any direct quotations.

3. Credit the source with a works cited section. (Refer to the documentation section of this chapter.)

4. Look over your paraphrase and check whether you have plagiarized. To avoid plagiarism, one of the following two actions must have occurred:

   a. either you quoted exactly, word for word, and recorded an endnote to give credit to the author (note: you were instructed not to use direct quotations—see point 2, above), or

   b. you paraphrased the author's idea in your own words, and recorded an endnote to give credit to the author. Most research papers contain a large number of endnotes.

EXERCISE

■ EXERCISE 2.3 WRITING AN ESSAY BASED ON ARTICLES

1. Your instructor will provide you with four newspaper articles dealing with a controversial subject. Read them.

2. Decide on a point of view (that is, an opinion, a slant, a thesis statement, or a central controlling idea).

3. Write a one-page, or shorter, essay using at least three of the four articles.

4. Use endnotes for the paraphrasing. (Refer to the documentation section in this chapter).

5. No direct quotations may be used.

6. Write a works cited section on a separate sheet of paper. The page numbers and the dates can be found on the articles.

7. For the proper endnote style to document your mini-essay, check the endnote section in this chapter.

8. Don't forget to include a brief introduction and conclusion. Reminder: To paraphrase is to take an idea from a source and to put that idea into your own words. In this case, the sources are four newspaper articles. The ideas belong to the newspaper staff who compiled the articles and they must be endnoted. If you don't, you have broken copyright laws and committed "academic dishonesty."

■ EXERCISE 2.4   RECOGNIZING BIAS AND SUMMARIZING

EXERCISE

Choose two current articles that deal with a particular issue in law enforcement. Make sure these articles are from different sources—for example, two different newspapers such as *The Toronto Star* and *The Globe and Mail*, or two different magazines such as *Maclean's* and *Elm Street*, or even a magazine and a newspaper, or an article from a reliable source on the Internet or from a CD-ROM. Although the articles discuss the same issue, they must express differing points of view. (For example, you could choose one article that supports mercy killing and another that condemns it.) The articles should be a minimum of 300 words, so that the issue is clearly discussed. If you choose a lengthy article, you may choose to summarize only the part(s) that express(es) the point of view you are examining.

1. Summarize each article following the guidelines discussed and practised in class, and make sure you don't add your own ideas.

Then, in essay form:

2. Present your own point of view and explain which article most closely supports it, and why.

3. Discuss the bias in each article and how the media and special interest groups use this bias to sway an uninformed audience.

4. Explain the importance of not allowing biases to interfere with the facts if you are a law enforcement officer and what you can do to avoid being influenced by your own beliefs or opinions.

5. Document the sources of your articles following the guidelines discussed in class. Refer to the documentation section of this chapter.

6. Include a photocopy of the articles with your summary and essay. If you chose a lengthy article, identify on the photocopy the part(s) of the article you are summarizing. The length of your summaries may vary depending on the length of the articles you have chosen, but your essay must be a minimum of one typed page, double-spaced.

(Exercise 2.4 is continued on the next page.)

(Exercise 2.4 continued ...)

Recognizing Bias and Summarizing Edit Sheet

Use the following checklist to make sure that you have followed all the instructions on the assignment sheet. For your assignment to be error-free, you should be able to answer "Yes" to each of the points listed below.

Two articles:	Yes ____	No ____	On same subject
	Yes ____	No ____	Different points of view
	Yes ____	No ____	Summarized
	Yes ____	No ____	Essay written
	Yes ____	No ____	Photocopies included and part(s) identified
	Yes ____	No ____	Sources documented
Summaries:	Yes ____	No ____	⅓ original length
	Yes ____	No ____	No direct quotations
	Yes ____	No ____	Written in own words
	Yes ____	No ____	Main ideas included
	Yes ____	No ____	No new ideas / interpretations
	Yes ____	No ____	Flows smoothly
	Yes ____	No ____	No grammar errors
	Yes ____	No ____	No spelling errors
Essay:	Yes ____	No ____	Presents own view
	Yes ____	No ____	Identifies supporting article
	Yes ____	No ____	Bias in each article
	Yes ____	No ____	How media use bias
	Yes ____	No ____	Why not to let media or your own bias as a law enforcement officer interfere
	Yes ____	No ____	How to avoid belief / opinion influence
	Yes ____	No ____	Flows smoothly
	Yes ____	No ____	No grammar errors
	Yes ____	No ____	No spelling errors
	Yes ____	No ____	Minimum of one typed page

■ **EXERCISE 2.5   EMPLOYMENT RESEARCH ESSAY**

EXERCISE

Select a specific agency, company, or organization (A/C/O) where you think you would like to work after graduation and thoroughly research that A/C/O.

Conduct at least one personal interview with an employee of the A/C/O. This may be with someone from human resources, an administrator, or a new or old employee. (It is always beneficial to get more than one point of view.) Also, gather information from two sources such as: the Internet, databases, CD-ROMs, library resources, pamphlets, and most recent annual reports.

To be sure you're prepared to write your research essay, make sure that you do the following:

◆ List the 20 questions to ask in an interview.

◆ Gather information such as the chief's or president's name and the A/C/O's history.

◆ Describe the areas the A/C/O services, the working conditions, and so on.

◆ Clearly explain the application process.

◆ Indicate the qualities sought in successful candidates.

◆ State the entry-level requirements.

◆ Explain the on- and/or off-site training.

◆ State the working hours and whether it is full- or part-time employment.

◆ Discuss the benefits provided by the A/C/O.

◆ Indicate the career opportunities within the A/C/O.

◆ Present the A/C/O's full name, address, and phone number.

◆ State the A/C/O's Web site address.

◆ State the name of your A/C/O contact person and his or her position or title.

Be prepared for the interview! You want to appear professional and prepared with pertinent questions. You may refer to the collecting information section below as you prepare your interview questions. Don't waste your contact's time inquiring about such things as the A/C/O's name, address, and phone number. Use your outside resource(s) to gather concrete information such as this before the interview.

(Exercise 2.5 is continued on the next page.)

(Exercise 2.5 continued ...)

Take notes during the interview so that you don't have to rely on memory for answers to your questions, and listen to your contact's answers because you may discover unanticipated information that you may wish to explore. Also, after the interview, be sure to thank your contact person.

Once you have completed your research, write a detailed 1000-word essay in which you present your information. As you write your essay, you may refer to the writing an essay section of this chapter. In your conclusion, based on the information you have presented, make an informed decision whether you would or would not like to work for this A/C/O. Be sure to support your conclusion with facts from the body of your essay.

Don't forget to submit your list of 20 interview questions with your essay, and don't forget to document all your sources of information.

On the day that you submit your employment research essay, you will be required to write a one-page summary of it in class. The writing style of your in-class summary must match that of your essay, and the information presented must be consistent with the information in your essay.

Use the Employment Research Essay Edit Sheet that follows to review each draft of your essay.

Employment Research Essay Edit Sheet

Content

For your essay to be error-free, you should be able to answer "Yes" to each of the points listed below.

Introduction:	Yes ____	No ____	Contains purpose/thesis statement
	Yes ____	No ____	Slant of the essay is apparent
	Yes ____	No ____	Indicates order of discussion of information
	Yes ____	No ____	Attracts the interest/attention of the reader
Body:	Yes ____	No ____	Clearly follows order stated in the introduction
	Yes ____	No ____	Each point addresses the main idea

(Exercise 2.5 is continued on the next page.)

(Exercise 2.5 continued ...)

	Yes ____	No ____	Each new idea is in a new paragraph
	Yes ____	No ____	Contains supporting details/examples
	Yes ____	No ____	Details/examples clearly apply to main ideas
	Yes ____	No ____	Facts are clearly presented
	Yes ____	No ____	Information is current and relevant
	Yes ____	No ____	Depth of research is apparent
	Yes ____	No ____	Quoted/paraphrased material is endnoted
Conclusion:	Yes ____	No ____	Summarizes information discussed
	Yes ____	No ____	Draws conclusions based on body of the essay
	Yes ____	No ____	Contains no unfounded ideas

Research

For your essay to meet the minimum requirements, you should be able to answer "Yes" to each of the points listed below.

Information:	Yes ____	No ____	Chief's or president's name
	Yes ____	No ____	A/C/O's history
	Yes ____	No ____	Areas the A/C/O services
	Yes ____	No ____	Working conditions
	Yes ____	No ____	Application process
	Yes ____	No ____	Qualities sought in successful applicants
	Yes ____	No ____	Entry-level requirements
	Yes ____	No ____	On- and/or off-site training
	Yes ____	No ____	Working hours
	Yes ____	No ____	Type of employment
	Yes ____	No ____	Benefits provided

(Exercise 2.5 is continued on the next page.)

(Exercise 2.5 continued ...)

Yes ____ No ____ Career opportunities within the A/C/O

Yes ____ No ____ A/C/O's complete name

Yes ____ No ____ A/C/O's address

Yes ____ No ____ A/C/O's phone number

Yes ____ No ____ A/C/O's Web site address

Yes ____ No ____ Contact person's name, position, extension

Yes ____ No ____ Decision to/not to pursue a job with this A/C/O

Yes ____ No ____ Information pertains to employment research

Yes ____ No ____ List of 20 questions included

Style

For your essay to be error-free, you should be able to answer "No" to each of the points listed below.

Grammar: Yes ____ No ____ Fragment sentences

Yes ____ No ____ Run-on sentences

Yes ____ No ____ Comma errors

Yes ____ No ____ Apostrophe errors

Yes ____ No ____ Parallelism errors

Yes ____ No ____ Wordiness errors

Spelling: Yes ____ No ____ Words misspelled

Yes ____ No ____ Homonyms used (see Writing Pitfalls, page 217)

Yes ____ No ____ Incorrect words for intended meaning

(Exercise 2.5 is continued on the next page.)

(Exercise 2.5 continued ...)

Documentation and Appearance

Don't concern yourself with this section until you have completed the final version of your essay. Only then is it necessary to consult the checklist below.

For your essay to be error-free, you should be able to answer "Yes" to each of the points listed below.

Works cited: Yes ____   No ____   Follows documentation guidelines (see the documentation section of this chapter)

Yes ____   No ____   Grammar/spelling error-free

Yes ____   No ____   On a separate page

Title page: Yes ____   No ____   Title of essay

Yes ____   No ____   Title in centre of page

Yes ____   No ____   Identification information in bottom right corner

Yes ____   No ____   Grammar/spelling error-free

Yes ____   No ____   On a separate page

Overall: Yes ____   No ____   Information is discussed in depth

Yes ____   No ____   Information is logically presented

Yes ____   No ____   Information flows smoothly

Yes ____   No ____   Essay is neatly typed

Yes ____   No ____   Typing is double-spaced

Yes ____   No ____   Essay is stapled

Interview Questions

For your interview questions to meet the requirements, you should be able to answer "Yes" to each of the points listed below.

Yes ____   No ____   20 questions

Yes ____   No ____   Organized logically

Yes ____   No ____   Pertain to your employment interests

Yes ____   No ____   Reflect depth of thought/research

Yes ____   No ____   Obtain detailed, specific information

CHAPTER 3
Non-Verbal Communication

KINESICS: THE STUDY OF BODY LANGUAGE

Kinesics, the study of body language, deals with non-verbal communication—that is, the actions and mannerisms that accompany or replace the spoken word. Whether or not you are aware of it, a person's first impression of you is made within the first four minutes of meeting, and much of that first impression is based on how you look and act. Once this first impression has been made, it is very hard to change it. Therefore, it's important that you project your best image right from the start.

As a police officer, you are expected to exude certain qualities including empathy, honesty, reliability, security, self-confidence, and safety. You are expected to be personable, polite, helpful, caring, strong, brave, outgoing, interested, concerned, physically fit, prompt, efficient, knowledgeable, and even clean and neat. Many of these things can be determined at a glance, and those that can't may be assumed because of how you look. In the following example, consider how those involved may judge you.

You arrive at a two-car accident within five minutes of getting the call. You immediately check for injuries, call for emergency vehicles, assist those who need help, and then interview the drivers, passengers, and bystanders.

From your actions, it may be observed that you are prompt, helpful, concerned, and knowledgeable. From what was observed, it may be inferred that you are caring, polite, strong, physically fit, and outgoing, and that you exude self-confidence and foster a sense of security. These are not characteristics attributed to you by people with whom you have had a lengthy conversation. Instead, they are opinions formed because of the way you acted and looked.

Do you know that you send a message even if you are silent? If you glare at a speaker while he or she is talking, what message are you sending? If you put your feet up, lie back in your chair, and pull your hat over your eyes, what message are you sending? If you glance at your watch a number of times, what message are you sending? You cannot *not* communicate!

Do you know that a non-verbal message outweighs a verbal one? If you insist that you're really interested in what someone is saying and yawn at the same time, which message will be believed? If you glare while you say that you don't mind if your girlfriend dates other guys, which message will be believed? If you slouch, laugh nervously, and hide your eyes under your hat while you express your self-confidence, which message will be believed? If your verbal and non-verbal messages conflict, the non-verbal messages are the ones that will be believed!

METHODS OF NON-VERBAL COMMUNICATION

You should be aware of different methods of non-verbal communication, both in yourself and in others. They include facial expressions, eye behaviour, gestures, body movements, posture, space or distance, touch, voice (pitch, rate, volume, hesitations, and pauses), physical appearance, and the use of time.

1. Facial Expressions and Eye Behaviour

Probably the most obvious forms of non-verbal communication are our facial expressions and eye contact. In most cultures, emotions are displayed by our facial expressions. Some of the emotions we show through our facial expressions are joy, sadness, surprise, interest, fear, and anger. Sometimes we try to hide our emotions. If something disturbs us, but we smile and laugh so that we don't show our anger, hurt, or embarrassment, we may be able to fool those we are with. However, our eyes might give us away.

Eye contact and intensity also show our emotions, but we tend to pay less attention to controlling our eye behaviour than our facial expressions. This is probably because we don't realize how much information is transmitted through a simple glance. Do you know that most liars have difficulty holding eye contact with the person to whom they are lying? Can you distinguish between a look of interest and a look of love?

We aren't born with the ability to understand facial expressions and eye behaviour; this is a learned and culturally bound ability. Different cultures, therefore, may interpret facial expressions and eye movements differently. For example, direct eye contact with an elder in an aboriginal community is generally considered rude. To be polite, one must glance at one's elder and look down. In other segments of Canadian culture, looking down generally shows disinterest and rudeness, and interest is shown through direct and often sustained eye contact. Because of these differences, it's important that you become aware of different cultures' interpretations of facial expressions and eye movements.

2. Gestures and Body Movements and Posture

Most of us are aware that our facial expressions tend to give away how we feel, so we try hard to contain our expressions. Instead, we often unconsciously express ourselves with our hands, arms, legs, and feet. Shifting our weight from foot to foot, fidgeting, rocking, scratching, and slouching all show our inattention or distraction. Though we try to hide our true feelings with a controlled facial expression, the movement of our body and limbs gives us away.

Body movements, posture, and gestures that show interest include leaning toward the speaker, sitting or standing straight, and nodding in agreement. Such movements show our interest not only in the speaker, but also in what is being said.

Like facial expressions and eye contact, such movements are culturally bound, and it's important that you learn to correctly interpret the gestures, body movements, and postures of different cultures. For example, in Canadian culture, a gesture used to show someone's height is to hold your hand out with your palm down. In some Asian cultures, this is considered an insult because it is a gesture used only for animals. To show someone's height in those cultures, you would hold your hand out with your palm up.

3. Space or Distance

The space we prefer around us, or the distance between ourselves and others, is culturally learned, and shows our relationship with others. In the majority Canadian culture, there are four basic distances. The first, from 0 in. to 18 in. (0 cm to 45 cm), is often referred to as intimate distance. At this distance you can touch, smell, and even feel the other person's closeness, and you are vulnerable since, if the need arises, it is not easy to move away quickly. Parents with young children, lovers, and very close friends or relatives can comfortably share this space without either person becoming uncomfortable. However, when an undesirable person approaches this closely, you may feel uneasy or even threatened.

The second distance, 18 in. to 4 ft. (45 cm to 1.2 m), is referred to as your personal distance. In this space you can reach out and touch the other person if you wish, but you welcome only some people into the space, and only at some times. Your acceptance of people at this distance depends largely upon the situation. At parties you may comfortably allow others to enter this space, but at work you may move back to prevent those same people from getting too close.

The third distance, 4 ft. to 12 ft. (1.2 m to 3.6 m), is referred to as social or business distance. This is the space within which most business is done. It may be in a small meeting, where you sit as close as 4 ft. apart, or a more formal situation in a conference room, where you may be 12 ft. from the farthest person. Here your senses don't pick up what they do at an intimate distance, but eye contact and body movement remain very important.

The fourth distance, beyond 12 ft. (3.6 m), is referred to as public distance. You experience this between yourself and a professor in a lecture theatre, and when you observe others from a distance. If you are in a deserted parking lot at night, and you feel uneasy about someone you see in the distance, public distance usually allows you the space to evade him or her or to defend yourself.

Once again, it is important to interpret the use of space or distance in different cultures.

4. Touch

The way you touch someone, or the way someone touches you, says a lot about your relationship and how comfortable you are with it. Usually, a hug, kiss, or an arm around the shoulder suggests an intimate relationship, and a friendly poke on the arm suggests a casual, friendly relationship. A handshake suggests something more formal, but still friendly and is often used at first encounters or in business situations.

Touch avoidance suggests that there is no relationship between people, or that the relationship is strained, and a punch or kick is usually the sign of dislike or anger.

In Canadian culture, who does the touching and the length of time you touch also depict the nature of your relationship. For example, if a parent gently puts his or her hand on a child's shoulder for just a second or two, it may be to comfort or to let the child know the parent is there. If, however, a girl puts her hand on her boyfriend's shoulder for a few seconds or more, it probably has a more intimate meaning.

Scratching, chewing your fingernails, and running your hands through your hair also tell others about you. These actions often indicate a lack of confidence or nervousness. They can certainly be distracting to others but are usually unconscious actions that can only be avoided once you become aware of them.

5. Voice

When you listen to someone's voice, there are five things that influence you. They are pitch, rate, volume, hesitation, and pauses. Pitch is how high or low someone's voice is. Usually the more excited someone becomes, the higher the pitch. Two other qualities influenced by excitement are rate and volume. The more excited or nervous someone becomes, the faster they tend to speak, and this is often accompanied by increased volume. Volume, however, is also used to intimidate others or to attract attention.

Hesitation tends to show that someone is unsure or, if questioned, doesn't know the answer or doesn't want to give a response. It is sometimes accompanied by starts and stops in the sentence. Hesitation sometimes has a negative effect on the listener because it is obvious that something is being avoided, and it, too, is a sign of nervousness. Pauses are different from hesitation. They may also be a sign of nervousness, but they tend to have a more positive effect on the listener. They suggest that the speaker is searching for the answer, catching his or her breath, or trying to organize his or her thoughts.

It is important to pay attention to all five aspects of both your voice and those aspects of others. Listen to them not individually but in conjunction with each other to truly hear what someone is saying.

6. Physical Appearance

Whether you know it or not, your appearance says a lot about you. As a police officer, you are expected to be neat and well groomed to set an example for others. If you are clean and neat, it suggests you care about yourself and that you probably care about others and your job.

If you are dirty and unkempt, overweight or too skinny, covered in tattoos you have made no effort to cover, have a strong body odour, or wear pierced earrings through your eyebrows, nose, lips, and tongue, it often makes people around you feel uncomfortable so that they won't even attempt to get to know the real you. No matter how much you insist that people will have to take you the way you are and for what you are, in the real world, where conservatism is the norm, it is unlikely that you will be accepted outside your peer group.

Other things that influence people's opinion of you are the colours you wear. More conservative colours are black, gray, and navy blue, whereas reds, yellows, and oranges make a much stronger statement. Also, colour combinations influence your impression on others.

Obviously, your clothes should match the activity you are performing. For example, if you're going to a police recruitment interview, you should dress appropriately for the appointment. Dressing in what you would wear for a night on the town, where you want to attract a hot date, probably isn't going to impress the personnel officer who will interview you. Also, be careful how much makeup you apply, how you style your hair, and how many rings and earrings you wear (and where you place them).

7. Use of Time

Different cultures treat time differently. In North America, we expect people to be on time; arriving late for an appointment or engagement is considered rude. Also, people are expected to get right down to business and not waste time on idle conversation. In contrast, in Japan, it is considered rude to delve into business without first exchanging pleasantries.

EXERCISE

■ EXERCISE 3.1 CULTURE AND COMMUNICATION

Like verbal communication, body language varies from culture to culture, and as police officers it is important that you are aware of the differences. As you look at the 10 statements below, consider the following questions and write brief answers in the spaces provided.

◆ What do the following statements suggest from the speaker's point of view?

◆ What could be the reason(s) for the other person's/people's action(s)?

1. He stands too close and crowds me when we speak.

2. I don't trust her; she never looks me in the eye.

3. I know he's uninterested because he always slouches in his chair and puts his feet on the desk when I'm talking to him.

(Exercise 3.1 is continued on the next page.)

(Exercise 3.1 continued ...)

4. She showed no emotion when I gave her the sad news about her father's death.

5. He's so pushy; he ignored the line and butt right in ahead of me.

6. It took forever for us to get down to work. First we had to make small talk, and once that was exhausted we finally got to the task at hand.

7. What is this world coming to? Did you see those two men kiss on the lips?

(Exercise 3.1 is continued on the next page.)

(Exercise 3.1 continued ...)

8. Last night I saw Manuel and Henoz walking down the street with their arms around each other. You'd think they could keep that behaviour to the privacy of their own home.

9. If looks could kill, I'd be dead right now.

10. It took only a glance from her mother to stop Tammy from misbehaving.

EXERCISE

■ EXERCISE 3.2   PHOTOGRAPHS

Introduction

What information can we capture at a glance, without hearing any words? Somehow, through our years of maturing, we have become almost experts in determining feelings, thoughts, and emotions by simply looking at a person. Most of us do this subconsciously, without really paying attention to how much body language we interpret on a daily basis.

Non-verbal language is a captivating field of study. Our species has been interested in the subject from the beginning of our history, whether we have been aware of it or not. Perhaps the appeal of Leonardo Da Vinci's "Mona Lisa" lies in the mystery of her smile, an intriguing expression that has captivated humans for centuries as we try to guess what her thoughts are.

Instructions

The class is divided into groups of four. Each group receives a folder containing a variety of photographs. Each group will answer the following questions on a separate sheet of paper:

1. Identify the emotions expressed in each photograph.

2. What relationships do you think exist in each scene?

3. List the non-verbal language that draws you to the above conclusions.

4. Present your findings to the class as a group, with each group member participating. Be prepared to support your ideas.

EXERCISE

■ EXERCISE 3.3 VIDEOTAPES

In class you will see a variety of short segments from videotapes. Each segment shows a range of situations and circumstances with a varying range emotions. The volume will be off during the viewing. Complete the chart below:

Identify:	Note non-verbal language that guided you to make these decisions:
The status of each actor	
The profession of each actor	
The emotions displayed by each actor	
The relationships between the actors	

■ EXERCISE 3.4   FREQUENCY OF NON-VERBAL LANGUAGE USE

EXERCISE

Introduction

Sometimes a person will say, "I never pay attention to non-verbal language. I concentrate on what people say." Whether you know it or not, you have used non-verbal language for many years to successfully make your way through life. Studying non-verbal language just makes you more aware and allows you to reap the benefits of being a good "people watcher."

Are you still not convinced of how often you use non-verbal language? Let's take a simple example of an action that every one of us performs frequently: passing a stranger as you walk along the sidewalk. To simplify this everyday activity even further, only eye contact will be considered.

Answer the Following Questions

1. What are the rules for eye contact as you approach each other?

2. If the passerby stares at you, what could it mean? It could probably mean a number of things.

3. Sometimes passersby end up in a little "dance" as they unintentionally block each other's way. What has happened in the communication process that results in such a "dance"?

(Exercise 3.4 is continued on the next page.)

(Exercise 3.4 continued ...)

4. Suppose a person walking past you on the sidewalk does not look at you. List possible things this person could be communicating.

5. Are the rules of eye contact for passersby the same regardless of location and time? For example: a large city at 02:30 hours versus a small town at 14:30 hours.

Humans are complex beings. As you can see, non-verbal signals relay important information, even in a common, daily event such as passing a stranger on the sidewalk.

EXERCISE

■ EXERCISE 3.5   VOICE

Introduction

Often it is not *what* we say but *how* we say it. Our words may say one thing, but our voices may give a different message.

Instructions

The instructor has eight pieces of paper in an envelope. Each piece of paper has a different emotion printed on it. Eight students will each select one of the pieces of paper and will keep its contents confidential. (Don't tell anyone which emotion you have selected!)

In this exercise there is one speaker. The speaker will ask a brief series of questions to each of the eight students. The questions will be the same in every case.

The class will pay attention to each student as their conversations take place. Although the speaker who asks the questions will

(Exercise 3.5 is continued on the next page.)

(Exercise 3.5 continued ...)

use the same tone of voice for each of the eight conversations, the eight volunteer students will carry on the conversation in a tone that matches the emotion recorded on his or her piece of paper. The class will guess what the emotion is.

The Conversation

Speaker: "Hello."
Student: "Hello."

Speaker: "How you are?"
Student: "Fine."

Speaker: "Anything wrong?"
Student: "No."

Speaker: "Are you sure?"
Student: "Yeah."

What have you learned about tone of voice from this exercise?

■ EXERCISE 3.6   THE ELEVATOR

EXERCISE

Upon receiving this non-verbal assignment, your body language will clearly indicate to the instructor how you feel about it. For example, you may feel a lack of enthusiasm, as well as discomfort, concerning this exercise.

As a new police constable, it takes time to become comfortable with being "nosy." To seek the truth when others do not want it revealed, and to persevere in an attempt to locate evidence, you must be persistent and tread where many citizens would not want to go.

This exercise will most likely make you feel uncomfortable because you were probably taught by your family to "mind your own business." The exercise provides you with experience in what it is like to be a police officer—*nosy!*

Instructions

Walk into a crowded elevator, ensuring that you are the last, or one of the last, to enter the elevator. Usually, when doing this, you would face the doors, with your back to the other occupants of the elevator. In this exercise, however, you will (bravely) face the others in the elevator, with your back to the doors.

Of course, you will feel uncomfortable, but there is a great deal to learn from such an exercise. Complete the following information:

(Exercise 3.6 is continued on the next page.)

(Exercise 3.6 continued ...)

1. Identify where the elevator is located, the occupants in the elevator, and the time of day.

2. Note the non-verbal language displayed by the occupants of the elevator during the brief (but long!) elevator ride.

3. What can you assume from the reactions of the people in the elevator? How do you think they were feeling? (These are not the same questions as number 2. Number 2 asked you to list the non-verbal language, whereas this question asks for your interpretation of that non-verbal language.)

4. If you conducted this experiment in a different type of building at a different time, do you think that the results would be different? For example: an office building at 09:00 hours versus a downtown hotel at 03:00 hours.

(Exercise 3.6 is continued on the next page.)

(Exercise 3.6 continued ...)

5. What did you learn about non-verbal behaviour from completing this assignment?

Having finished this exercise, do you think that it will take you a period of time to become comfortable with being "nosy?"

■ **EXERCISE 3.7   OFFICER SAFETY AND NON-VERBAL LANGUAGE**

EXERCISE

Instructions

1. Watch the video *Officer Safety*. The volume will be turned off.

2. Record the body language of the actors in each scenario on the following chart. Examples are provided.

3. Record what you believe the non-verbal language tells us. Examples are provided. Bear in mind the title of the video.

4. Record what you think the scene is about. Again, examples are provided.

5. At the end of the exercise, the video will be replayed with the volume on, in order than you might see how accurate your observations were.

Note to the instructor: The video *Officer Safety* is part of the Tactical Training Series published in 1987 by AIMS Media of Scarborough, Ontario. The scenes unfold quickly. In order to capture all of the details, each segment may need to be replayed a number of times.

(Exercise 3.7 is continued on the next page.)

(Exercise 3.7 continued ...)

Record aspects of body language of all of the actors	What you think the body language says	What you think the scene is about
1. Officer attending an alarm call. As the officer pulls up the driveway to a premises, his facial expression is serious and he has direct eye contact focused on the building even before he gets out of the car. He walks slowly toward the building with one hand in his pocket. His intent eye contact continues as he walks along the side of the building. After he has walked halfway down the building, his facial expression and body posture change. His lips purse in a bit of a grimace, he moves his head slightly upward, his body relaxes, and he turns back, walking in the direction from which he came.	The officer appears alert as he drives into the parking lot. His strong eye contact from the start shows his interest. As he walks along the wall, he still looks interested, although I wonder why he has his one hand in his pocket, especially his right hand. (If he is right-handed and something suddenly happens, he has a disadvantage since his right hand is in his pocket). He stops part way along the wall and suddenly changes his body and facial expression. To me, his body language says: "Here we go again, another waste of time." He does not check the remainder of the perimeter.	I wonder why the officer did not finish checking the building exterior. At first, the officer displays an interest in the call, but soon that interest melts away. Since I can't hear the sound, I don't know what changed his mind so quickly.
2. Routine traffic stops. **2a.** This officer doesn't get much of a chance before he is shot. I didn't see much activity on the part of the officer because the scene unfolded so quickly. I saw the driver quickly get out of his car, shoot the officer, and then walk toward the officer very slowly and cautiously. His arms were extended straight out as he continued to point the gun at the officer; his face was very serious and his shoulders rounded.	I couldn't really see much with the officer exiting his unit, but perhaps he might have noticed the driver's sudden quick movements and at least attempted to dive for cover. As the driver slowly walked toward the officer lying motionless on the ground, it seemed to me as if the driver was expecting the officer to spring up at any moment and defend himself. The driver seemed nervous.	Obviously, this scene is about a serious shooting of an officer. I can see how quickly it can happen.

(Exercise 3.7 is continued on the next page.)

(Exercise 3.7 continued ...)

Record aspects of body language of all of the actors	What you think the body language says	What you think the scene is about
2b. This second officer pulling over the car has strong eye contact with the car that he has pulled over. As he stares at the vehicle, his facial expression is serious. He checks the rear-view mirror and over his shoulder before exiting the police vehicle. He seems to use caution as he approaches the car; his alert, upright body posture shows this. His body movements seem guarded and he walks close to the pulled-over vehicle. When he reaches the driver's door he does not stand right next to the door. His eyes are trained on the driver. As he speaks to the driver, his body leans slightly forward. The driver of the vehicle has a calm facial expression and his body movements seem relaxed as he produces his i.d. for the officer.	He looks very cautious, judging by his facial expression, his body movements, and his postures. I think he stares intently at the stopped vehicle, trying to assess the situation. I think that he checks the rear-view mirror and over his shoulder before he exits his unit so that he will not strike, or be struck by, any oncoming traffic or cyclist(s). When he walks closely next to the stopped car, it almost seems that he plans to use it for cover, should anything happen. He carefully positions his body a certain distance from the driver's vehicle. I get the impression that he is waiting for something to happen, like maybe the driver will open the car door and try to hit him with the door. The driver seems cooperative and "normal," as well as polite.	When I see how cautious the officer is, I think that this episode may be about taking the time to be careful. This officer seems to be taking no chances. Thinking back to the first officer, who was shot, I remember that he did not pause to take a good look at the driver and the situation before he exited his car. Maybe the outcome would have been different if he had done that. I also think the video is warning you that it just isn't humans who may harm you. Oncoming traffic can be just as deadly.

(Exercise 3.7 is continued on the next page.)

(Exercise 3.7 continued ...)

Record aspects of body language of all of the actors	What you think the body language says	What you think the scene is about
2c. This officer walks slowly and cautiously toward the stopped car, with his eyes focused on the driver. When he gets near the car, he leans over as if he intends to speak to the driver, but he is still not near the driver's door. The driver has an expressionless face as he locates and produces his i.d. for the officer.	This officer is being careful and watching out for his safety. The driver shows no facial expression and no hint that he may use a weapon against the officer. I think the driver is checking to find the location of the weapon, and may be wondering whether to use it.	I think that this scene is showing the viewers that every small movement should be noticed. I want to hope that there is a way that the officer could notice that something dangerous might happen, so that the officer might be able to protect himself. Maybe the officer might wonder why the driver's right arm and hand are moving to his right side and behind his back. The driver has already produced his i.d., so why is the driver moving in this fashion? If the officer were able to notice this movement, then the officer would have a warning. This scenario makes me think that because this "bad guy" seems to cooperate with the officer and looks "normal," maybe the officer will drop his guard.

(Exercise 3.7 is continued on the next page.)

(Exercise 3.7 continued ...)

Record aspects of body language of all of the actors	What you think the body language says	What you think the scene is about
3. Officer writing out a ticket while standing on the sidewalk.		
4. Officer on sidewalk dealing with bearded male wearing dress shirt and pants.		

(Exercise 3.7 is continued on the next page.)

(Exercise 3.7 continued ...)

Record aspects of body language of all of the actors	What you think the body language says	What you think the scene is about
5. Officer carrying out a sobriety test with a female.		
6. Officer talking to citizen on sidewalk.		

(Exercise 3.7 is continued on the next page.)

(Exercise 3.7 continued ...)

Record aspects of body language of all of the actors	What you think the body language says	What you think the scene is about
7. Officer sitting in unit; citizen approaches.		
8. Two officers dealing with male fixing motorcycle.		

(Exercise 3.7 is continued on the next page.)

(Exercise 3.7 continued ...)

Record aspects of body language of all of the actors	What you think the body language says	What you think the scene is about
9. Male officer arresting female driver.		
10. Officer standing on sidewalk with drunken male wearing flowered Hawaiian shirt.		

(Exercise 3.7 is continued on the next page.)

(Exercise 3.7 continued ...)

Record aspects of body language of all of the actors	What you think the body language says	What you think the scene is about
11. Police officer arriving at business office.		
12. Officer talking to male at wrought-iron gates.		

(Exercise 3.7 is continued on the next page.)

(Exercise 3.7 continued ...)

Record aspects of body language of all of the actors	What you think the body language says	What you think the scene is about
13. Officer exiting unit and approaching male on sidewalk in front of store.		
14. Officer signalling male near high wooden gate.		

(Exercise 3.7 is continued on the next page.)

(Exercise 3.7 continued ...)		
Record aspects of body language of all of the actors	**What you think the body language says**	**What you think the scene is about**
15. Officer in bar with two intoxicated females and bartender.		
16. Two officers dealing with two citizens.		*(Exercise 3.7 is continued on the next page.)*

(Exercise 3.7 continued ...)

Record aspects of body language of all of the actors	What you think the body language says	What you think the scene is about
17. Elderly man arguing with male worker behind counter.		
18. Return to scene of the two officers talking to the male fixing motorcycle.		

(Exercise 3.7 is continued on the next page.)

(Exercise 3.7 continued ...)		
Record aspects of body language of all of the actors	**What you think the body language says**	**What you think the scene is about**
19. Officer exiting from car.		
20. Officer pulling up in unit in alley, approaching male standing by truck.		

(Exercise 3.7 is continued on the next page.)

(Exercise 3.7 continued ...)

Debriefing

1. The police officers in the video usually displayed one facial expression. Describe that expression.

2. Studies show that if an individual in the general population has an elevated interest in someone, then that individual will look at the subject with about 60 to 64 percent eye contact. This high percentage of eye contact indicates a high interest.

   a. In the video, what would you estimate was the percentage of eye contact displayed by the police officers toward the subjects they were dealing with?

   b. Why do you think that police officers display this percentage of eye contact?

3. Perhaps you have heard the expression, "You can always spot an off-duty police officer." Describe the body language that off-duty officers display that may reveal their occupation.

(Exercise 3.7 is continued on the next page.)

(Exercise 3.7 continued ...)

4. In scenarios 12 and 17, you saw two physical confrontations. Were these physical confrontations similar to the ones that you see on television or in the movies? Which version of physical confrontations do you think is the realistic one?

5a. The first few times that you watched the video, the sound was turned off. Did you notice the typed messages on the screen?

5b. When the video was replayed with the sound turned on, did you notice the typed message as much as when the sound was turned off? Explain your answer.

6. What have you learned about officer safety and non-verbal language from this exercise? Write your answer in the space below, as if you were shown this video in a police testing situation and asked the question. If necessary, you may use additional lined paper.

(Exercise 3.7 is continued on the next page.)

(Exercise 3.7 continued ...)

Caution: In your answer, don't forget about everything that you have been taught about writing an essay. The testers will not remind you to include an introduction and a conclusion. Of course, you know that spelling and grammar errors are a definite no-no!

(Exercise 3.7 continued ...)

EXERCISE

■ **EXERCISE 3.8   NON-VERBAL COMMUNICATION**

Purpose

◆ To increase your skill in observing non-verbal behaviour.

◆ To provide you with experience in a surveillance activity.

◆ To illustrate the dangers of being too confident that you are a perfect reader of body language.

◆ To increase your awareness of your own body language.

Step 1

Select a subject. Do not let this person or anyone else know whom you have selected. You will learn more from this assignment if you select a person you do not know very well.

For three days observe only your subject's behaviour. How does he or she move, what are his or her mannerisms and postures, speech, dress, and so on? Record your observations. Note: Observe your subject only; do not follow him or her.

Do not interpret your subject's actions; simply record what you see. For example, recording that "subject looks tired" is not an observation of body language but an interpretation. (For an explanation of the differences among facts, hearsay, inferences, and opinions, see the chart on page 138.) The interpretation that the subject is tired is based on body language such as:

◆ rubbing eyes,

◆ eye lids droopy,

◆ body slouching in chair, shoulders rounded,

◆ eyes staring off into distance,

◆ subject not looking at person talking to him or her,

◆ dark circles below eyes, and

◆ eyes squinting in high-intensity light.

The above observations of a subject may be interpreted to indicate that the subject is tired. However, interpretations are not part of step 1. Record only your observations. (Interpretations are part of step 2.) Examples of categories sought for in step 1 include

◆ gestures, body movements, facial expressions, eyes, eyebrows, posture;

◆ clothing, colours, hair, jewelry, makeup;

(Exercise 3.8 is continued on the next page.)

(Exercise 3.8 continued ...)

- ◆ voice (paralanguage) including pitch, rate, volume, hesitations, pauses;

- ◆ space and distance;

- ◆ the use of time; and

- ◆ touch.

The following chart provides an example of how you might make your notes for step 1. Note that observations for days 1 to 3 do not have to be made on consecutive days, in effect, one day after the other.

■ Step 1: Record behaviour only

Day 1	Day 2	Day 3

(Exercise 3.8 is continued on the next page.)

(Exercise 3.8 continued ...)

Step 2

For the next three days, you will not only observe and note your subject's actions, but you will also attempt to interpret them. For example, your subject has been yawning a great deal. You may conclude that he or she is bored, tired from a late night, or had a large meal and is sleepy.

Examples of interpretations sought for in step 2 include:

◆ What does the communicator's facial expression reveal? Are facial expressions relatively consistent or fleeting, and what might be the significance of this? Do they fluctuate drastically, and what might be the significance of this? Assess the extent to which you believe the facial expressions are genuine.

◆ Analyze and interpret body cues, hand and foot movements, and body motion. During an interaction with another party, does your subject move too much or too little? Are both people interested in the exchange? Is your subject or the other party more eager to continue the communication? How do you know?

◆ Assess the extent to which your subject mirrors the postures of others. How does posture support or contradict the status of the relationship that exists? Is your subject relaxed or tense? Why? Has your subject used his or her body to include or exclude others from conversations? Analyze when or why your subject alters his or her posture.

◆ Watch your subject's eyes. Does he or she look away more than the other person? Is there excessive blinking? Staring? How does the eye contact of your subject appear to affect the other person? When is your subject's eye contact most pronounced?

◆ Is the volume of your subject's voice and the speech rate appropriate, given the particular situation? Does the voice support or contradict what is being said? Analyze how and when silence is used. Be responsive to signals of nervousness and changes in pitch.

◆ Does your subject touch people? Why does he or she touch a particular person and not another? How did touching or being touched affect your subject? Was the contact appropriate or inappropriate to the situation? Why?

The following chart provides an example of how you might make your notes for step 2. Note that observations for days 4 to 6 do not have to be made on consecutive days (that is, one day after the other).

(Exercise 3.8 is continued on the next page.)

(Exercise 3.8 continued ...)

■ Step 2: Record behaviour plus interpretations

Day 4	Day 5	Day 6

(Exercise 3.8 is continued on the next page.)

(Exercise 3.8 continued ...)

Step 3

At the completion of this three-day period, meet with your subject to discuss the behaviour you observed as well as your interpretations. How accurate were your observations? How did you feel about the assignment? Have your subject provide feedback by completing the checklist below.

Feedback Checklist

The following feedback list for step 3 should be completed by the subject.

1. All aspects of non-verbal language were covered in the student's notes—namely, gestures, body movements, facial expressions, eyes, eyebrows, posture, clothing, colours, hair, jewelry, makeup, voice, space and distance, the use of time, and touch.   Y   N

2. The person watching me remained undetected and was good at covert activities.   Y   N

3. I was surprised at how many actions I performed without being aware of them.   Y   N

4. I didn't know how many habits I had.   Y   N

5. In the future I will probably be more conscious of what my body is saying.   Y   N

6. I was upset with the student for watching me when I didn't know. In a way, I felt as if my privacy were being invaded.   Y   N

7. The student picked out something about me that no one knew about, since I had not told anyone. In other words, he or she learned a truth from my non-verbal language.   Y   N

8. Now I am going to start paying greater attention to what other people are saying with their bodies.   Y   N

9. The student misinterpreted my non-verbal behaviour most of the time.   Y   N

10. The student was accurate about my feelings about half of the time.   Y   N

11. The student was accurate about my feelings most of the time.   Y   N

(Exercise 3.8 is continued on the next page.)

(Exercise 3.8 continued ...)

Step 4

Two weeks following the date on which the exercise was assigned, each student will bring to class:

1. detailed rough notes from step 1,

2. detailed rough notes from step 2,

3. findings from step 3 and the checklist completed by your subject.

Step 5

In class, you will write a short, formal essay containing the conclusions you drew after carrying out this exercise. Your topic will be: "What I learned about non-verbal language by carrying out this assignment." Attendance on this date is mandatory.

You will write the essay in class, during regularly scheduled class time. You are encouraged to bring a dictionary with you, plus an outline to help with your writing. Essays will be double-spaced.

Since this is an exercise in writing, do not use subheadings or subtitles. (Join the essay with words, not subheadings or subtitles.)

In this assignment your rough notes from steps 1 and 2 are essential and worth half of your mark. Ensure that your notes are detailed enough and are brought to class for submission to the teacher.

Contact the instructor before essay day if you have any problems with these instructions.

EXERCISE

■ EXERCISE 3.9   HOW DO YOU DEPICT CONFIDENCE IN A JOB INTERVIEW?

Instructions

1. The class will be divided into groups of three speakers.

2. Groups 1 to 6 will follow the script provided for the job interview role play. The roles involve that of:

    a. the interviewer,

    b. a job applicant depicting confident non-verbal behaviour, and

    c. a job applicant depicting a lack of confidence in his or her body language.

    Each group will demonstrate two scenes.

3. Look at the list on pages 38 to 41 of this text. It outlines the aspects included in non-verbal behaviour. These aspects will be considered as each group prepares its role play. They combine to give a picture of a person showing either confidence or a lack of confidence.

4. The first scene will display a job candidate who shows either confidence or a lack of confidence.

5. The second scene will demonstrate the opposite of the first scene.

6. Can the audience guess which scene is which?

Note: The same script will be used for each role play. In other words, the only difference between the two candidates will be their actions, not their words. The words will be the same. Only the non-verbal aspects will vary.

Role Plays

Group 1/Question 1

Interviewer: Describe what you have to offer this organization.

Interviewee: I have great communication skills and I am an organized person. I work well with others and cooperate with my supervisors. I am also dependable.

Group 2/Question 2

Interviewer: Why should we hire you?

Interviewee: I have lots of experience in this area. I enjoy this type of work and am good at it.

(Exercise 3.9 is continued on the next page.)

(Exercise 3.9 continued ...)

Group 3/Question 3

Interviewer: I understand that you had a summer job with the Grand River Conservation Authority as a security guard. Could you tell me a bit about the job?

Interviewee: I learned a lot on the job. One night I had to chase a trespasser through the park and ended up having to hit him. Another time I ordered a large group of disorderlies out of the park. There were about 25 of them. I also had to help the police one night when they arrested a man for a stabbing. I got to handcuff him.

Group 4/Question 4

Interviewer: What has been your most rewarding career experience?

Interviewee: My most rewarding experience was field placement with a regional police service. I encountered many different situations and I observed a variety of ways to effectively handle each situation.

Group 5/Question 5

Interviewer: If you had a choice, what type of job would you want?

Interviewee: I want a reasonable paying job that I don't have to take home with me unless I want to.

Group 6/Question 6

Interviewer: For what types of jobs has your training prepared you?

Interviewee: My training has prepared me for any position in the law and security field.

Task for Groups 7 Through 9

This part of the exercise examines what would be considered good answers to certain job interview questions.

1. Read the scripted responses of the interviewees to the questions.

2. Comment on the answers.

3. Improve any answers that you feel are weak or poor.

4. Present your results to the class.

    a. Group 7 examines questions 1 and 2.

    b. Group 8 examines questions 3 and 4.

    c. Group 9 examines questions 5 and 6.

CHAPTER 4
Oral Presentations

WHY STUDY PUBLIC SPEAKING?

1. It Increases Your Personal and Social Abilities

Public speaking provides training for a variety of personal and social competencies. For example, it improves your self-confidence and self-awareness, and helps you overcome the fear of communicating both one on one and with large groups.

2. It Enhances Your Academic and Career Skills

Skills that are central to public speaking are skills that can also be used in other situations. For example, they improve your ability to

◆   research information,

◆   explain matters clearly,

◆   support an argument using methods of persuasion,

◆   present yourself with confidence, and

◆   analyze and evaluate the validity of arguments and persuasive appeals.

3. It Refines Your General Communication Abilities

Public speaking improves your general communication abilities by helping you to

◆   develop a more effective communication style,

◆   enhance your confidence,

◆   adjust messages to specific listeners,

◆   detect and respond to feedback,

◆   develop logical and emotional appeal,

◆   build and communicate your credibility,

- ◆ enhance your assertiveness,

- ◆ improve your listening skills, and

- ◆ refine your delivery skills.

4. It Improves Your Public-Speaking Abilities

Good speakers are not born, but created through hard work. Make sure your topic is interesting and appropriate for both you and your audience, in order to make it worthwhile. This requires research, planning, organization, and practice. These four things will help you improve as a speaker, as a listener, and as a critic.

MAKING ORAL PRESENTATIONS

As a police officer, you never know when you will be called upon to speak to the public. You may need to explain a traffic law to a motorist caught speeding, or you may need to instruct a group of people on how to safeguard themselves and their homes against a rash of break-ins. You won't always be given a day or a week to prepare.

The general public expects certain qualities of you, such as honesty, concern for their well-being, a thorough knowledge of your topic, the ability to explain things in laypeople's terms, confidence, and the sense of security and control you project, stemming from these qualities. Even if you don't have time to prepare, you can demonstrate the foregoing qualities if you treat your topic and your audience seriously.

When you are given time to prepare, oral presentations aren't difficult. You simply need to learn the basic techniques. The most important thing to remember is that, for most people, perfecting presentations requires a lot of practice.

The first thing you need to do is choose a topic if one hasn't been assigned. Once you've done this, brainstorm all its aspects. From the list you create, limit your information to the important points you can cover in the time you're allowed. Make sure you narrow your points so that you can clearly and thoroughly discuss them in the allotted time. For example, if you're to speak for three to five minutes, you'll probably have only three or four main points to discuss. By the time you've introduced your topic, discussed it, and stated your conclusion, you'll probably find you've spoken long enough.

Always keep your audience in mind. Speaking to a group of law enforcement officers is often much different from speaking to the general public. The language you use, the information you supply, and even the way you present the information will be influenced by your listeners and their backgrounds.

After you narrow your topic, decide which supporting material clarifies your points. You may include examples or facts to support your point of view, and you may appeal to your audience's emotions. After you gather all your information, you need to organize it in a way that's easy for you to present and for the listeners to understand.

Sometimes it helps to write your speech out in full, making sure it flows logically. Other times it is sufficient to record only the main points and supporting details. Methods of presentation include chronological order, cause and effect, and sequential order.

Practise reading your speech both silently and aloud. Listen as you read the words to make sure that what you say supports your topic, makes sense, and flows smoothly. Then read the speech to someone who will listen critically and help you with any content or structural difficulties. (It's usually not a good idea to ask your best friend, who doesn't want to hurt your feelings!)

When you feel confident that the content and structure are clear and cohesive, rewrite your speech in point form. This time, write only the introduction and conclusion out in full, if you need to. Practise saying the speech both silently and aloud, filling in the missing words. Try not to read, but instead pretend you are talking to someone. Try to use a conversational tone. When you feel comfortable, say your speech to someone else. Each time you present, your critical audience should watch for, and comment on, one of the five important presentation skills that follow. (Don't expect your audience to watch for all five skills at once.)

FIVE IMPORTANT PRESENTATION SKILLS

There are five main things to be aware of when you actually make a presentation: clarity, confidence, content, stance, and fillers.

1. Clarity

The clarity of your presentation rests on three things.

1. You must make sure you enunciate clearly, so that your words aren't slurred, and you must be able to easily pronounce all the words you use. If you have always had trouble pronouncing a word, this is not the place to use it. Instead, use another word or phrase that doesn't cause you difficulty. Also, use words that your audience can understand. Buzz words and jargon may be understood by you and your fellow officers, but the general public may be completely baffled by them.

2. You must project your voice so that you can easily be heard by everyone in your audience. That doesn't mean that you should shout, but you must be prepared to talk above noises such as fans, machines, and other external distractions. Remember, when you're at a traffic accident, you won't have ideal conditions for issuing your instructions.

3. You need to vary your speed, pitch, and volume. No one speaks at a constant rate, in a monotone, and without getting louder or softer. (Even computer voice simulation takes these things into account.) Varying the way you speak is how you show enthusiasm for your subject. Usually, if you are excited about something, you speak more quickly, at a higher pitch, and more loudly. Remember, though, that this is an oral presentation, and you shouldn't race through your speech in a squeaky, loud voice.

Vary your pitch and you will more easily involve your audience. Remember, however, that when you're nervous you may tend to speak in a higher voice, so you may need to concentrate on lowering your voice. This is especially important when you reach the end of a sentence, because if you end on a high note, it sounds as though you are asking a question or are unsure of yourself and are asking for acceptance or permission. It is important that you sound as though you are in control.

Vary your volume to naturally show your enthusiasm for your topic and your interest in sharing it with your audience. Sometimes, when you're nervous, you may tend to speak in almost a whisper. At first the audience may strain to hear what you're saying, but usually they quickly lose interest and become distracted. Make a conscious effort to speak loudly enough that everyone can hear. In regular conversation, we automatically speak a little more loudly when we're excited about something, so use this to your advantage in your presentation. Don't yell at your audience, though—use your volume to involve them!

2. Confidence

Many people say their worst fear is getting up in front of an audience, particularly an audience of their peers, to speak. Therefore, when they're expected to appear confident while presenting, they feel they've been asked to do the impossible. There are five easy ways to appear calm and confident when you present.

1. Don't write out your entire speech. You may wish to write the introduction and conclusion in full, but write only the main ideas of the body in point form. Make sure your points are large enough, ordered, and spaced clearly so that you can easily see them at a glance. You may even wish to number them. For example, if you are giving the physical description of a person, the points for the body of your presentation could look something like the following.

a.	Sex	e.	Hair
b.	Height	f.	Eyes
c.	Weight	g.	Clothing
d.	Build	h.	Outstanding feature(s)

A list like the one above gives direction to your speech and helps to keep you ordered and on track, but you can't simply read the information. Not letting yourself read it forces you to talk to your audience. Remember, those you are speaking to can usually read as well as you can, so if all you're going to do is read to them, you're better to hand them a typed presentation.

2. Use cue cards. Put your points on cards no larger than 3 by 5 inches. Large sheets of paper often encourage you to record too much information, and this entices you to read. There is also the tendency to hold a sheet of paper up in front of you (so you can hide behind it). It is very distracting for the audience to watch, and listen to, a piece of paper as it shakes in the hands of a nervous speaker.

    Leave your cue cards on the lectern or desk in front of you so you aren't tempted to fidget, but so you may refer to them if you need direction. Make sure that you number your cue cards so you can confirm that they're in the correct order.

3. Look at your audience. In some public-speaking classes, students are taught to look just over the heads of their audience. Unless you are in a packed auditorium, this is usually obvious and ineffective. Others are taught to imagine everyone in the audience in his or her underwear; however, most people fail to find this relaxing. To show your honesty and sincerity, you need to make eye contact. This does not mean that you stare at someone in the audience, but that you look at each person (depending on the audience size) for two to three seconds. Remember not to do this row by row, but do cover the entire audience and not just one little corner of your friends. By doing this, you engage your listeners.

4. Try to avoid the nervous giggle. Often this appears to be an "in" joke with someone in the audience, and the others not only feel left out but usually tune out. If you look up or at someone and feel you are going to laugh, look away and pause for a moment while you compose yourself.

5. Try to avoid sighing. Although you may simply be taking or releasing a deep breath, to your audience it may appear that you are bored with your topic. Remember that you control your audience's interest, and if you seem to be uninterested, they will soon follow suit.

3. Content

Content is the substance of your presentation, and there are three parts. You need a clear beginning, middle, and end. This is sometimes referred to as the tell, tell, tell method of presenting.

1. The beginning is your introduction. Here you catch your audience's attention and introduce your topic. You give direction to your presentation so that your audience can anticipate what is coming

next. The introduction is usually only two or three sentences long, unless you begin by telling a story or joke. Remember, you must tell your audience what you are going to discuss!

2. The middle is the body, where you present your findings, give instructions, relate facts, give proof, supply details, and so forth. In essence, it's where you support your point of view in a logical, orderly manner. You may wish to number your points, or you may choose to use transition words or phrases, such as "also," "furthermore," "as well," "another," and "the next," to let your audience know that you are moving to a new point. Here you tell your audience about your topic and support your point of view.

3. The end is your conclusion. It lets your audience know that you are finished, and it may begin with such phrases as, "In conclusion ..." or "As a result ... ." If your audience's concentration has waned, statements such as these will often catch their attention again so that they will listen to the gist of your presentation. The conclusion should be a brief restatement of your point of view and a summary of your main points, and it may address your audience directly. It does not contain any new ideas! It is here that you briefly tell your audience what you have already said.

4. Stance

The way you stand and address your audience is as important as what you have to say. People believe 93 percent of what they see and 7 percent of what they hear, so how you look will affect how your message is received. This involves body language, and the way you appear to treat your subject will influence the way it will be treated by your audience. There are six points to remember about body language.

1. Try to look relaxed without looking too casual. Stand straight but not like a tin soldier. It's OK to rest your hands on the lectern or desk, provided that you don't lean on it, or drape yourself over it. If you place one foot slightly ahead of the other, and put more weight on your front foot, you move toward your audience and look more interested and involved. (If you stand on your back foot, it may appear that you want to get away and are uncomfortable in the situation.)

2. Stand still and avoid the tendency to rock, swing, or sway. Such actions sometimes occur when you grab the lectern for security and realize that it moves. Once you get into a rhythm, it's almost impossible to stop, and it can become a major distraction for your audience. You may move around at the front of the room, or move toward your audience, but don't pace as though you're anxious.

3. Understand that it's okay to use your hands to gesture, but don't wave your arms around so that they detract from what you are

saying. Keep your hands still unless you are gesturing. Try not to fidget with pens or papers you have with you, and don't play with keys or coins in your pockets. If you have an itch, deal with it before you present, and ignore it while you are speaking. If you have long hair, fasten it off your face before you speak so you won't need to constantly push it out of the way.

Remember the effect that gestures have on your listeners. While some may be comforting and natural, and therefore go unnoticed, others, such as shaking your fist or slamming something down on a desk, may startle or intimidate your audience.

4. Make sure that you smile. You are supposed to be interested in sharing your information with your audience, so look as if you are.

5. Make sure that your audience can see your face. Remove your hat before you present, and again, tie your hair off your face. Remember, your audience needs to see your eyes!

6. Dress appropriately for your presentation. Whether you are wearing your uniform, a business suit, or casual attire, make sure that you and your clothes are neat and clean, and don't wear too much makeup. People form a first impression of you on the basis of your appearance.

5. Fillers

A well-rehearsed presentation does not contain fillers. These are words or expressions such as "um," "ah," "like," and "you know." They simply take up space and add nothing to the content of your speech. It's much better to pause while you collect your thoughts than to fill the void with useless words.

The use of fillers is probably the clearest indication that you are unprepared, and they show your lack of professionalism and consideration for your audience. Therefore, it is important that you practise, practise, practise to avoid using distracting filler words.

EXERCISE

(Exercise 4.1 is continued on the next page.)

■ **EXERCISE 4.1   PREPARING FOR PUBLIC SPEAKING**

Think back to your experience as a listener:

1. Describe the behaviour of the most effective speaker you have ever listened to.

2. Contrast the above description with a description of the most ineffective speaker you have listened to.

3. What interests you when listening to a speech?

(Exercise 4.1 continued ...)

4. What bores you?

5. What things do you notice about a speaker?

6. Good speakers know their strengths and limitations. Identify yours below.

DEMONSTRATION SPEECH

Many times in your career as a police officer, you'll be asked to explain something to people, and there is no better way than to both show them and tell them at the same time. A demonstration speech does exactly that. First, it shows your audience how to do something, and second, it tells them how to do it. You must remember that it is both a demonstration and a speech, so you must do both things at once; therefore, you must continually talk as you demonstrate.

Although, as a police officer, you probably won't be asked to explain something like the example below, a good way to start speaking in public is to begin with something that is simple and familiar. That way, you don't need to concentrate on the content and you can spend more time working on your presentation skills.

The following is a sample demonstration speech. The first version is written out in full, so it is easy to follow and practise. The presenter could use this to practise the five important presentation skills until he or she feels comfortable. Notice that it's written to be spoken, not to be read by the audience. It has a conversational tone, and the introduction is intended to attract attention, while the conclusion offers a quick review.

Milkshake Presentation I

Introduction

Good morning/afternoon. I've just come from a fast food restaurant, where I had the *worst* milkshake I've ever had, and I *know* I make much better ones at home. So can you. I'll show you how.

Body

First, you need the following ingredients:

◆ ice cream,

◆ vanilla,

◆ Ovaltine, and

◆ milk.

Then you need:

◆ a blender,

◆ an ice cream scoop or large spoon,

◆ a teaspoon, and

◆ a tablespoon.

Into the blender place 6 scoops of ice cream. Add 1 teaspoon of vanilla and 2 to 3 tablespoons of Ovaltine, depending on your taste. Finally, pour in enough milk to cover the ice cream. That's about 1 pint.

Note: For audiences who are more familiar with the metric system, the measurements would be given as follows:

Into the blender place 6 scoops of ice cream. Add 5 ml of vanilla and 30 to 45 ml of Ovaltine, depending on your taste. Finally, pour in enough milk to cover the ice cream. That's about half a litre.

Now make sure you put the lid on tightly, and check to make sure that the blender is plugged in. Turn the blender on and off quickly 3 or 4 times to mix things up, and then let the blender run on high for a couple of minutes.

Conclusion

(While the blender is mixing, repeat the instructions. Step into the audience so that everyone can hear.)

Well, it looks as if it's ready. Who'd like to be the first to try it?

Although the second version of the presentation, which follows, is not yet written on cue cards, it is written in point form. This gives the presenter the freedom to change the wording as the speech progresses. Notice that the introduction and conclusion are still written in full, just in case the presenter suddenly gets nervous and doesn't know what to say. (Even though all the words are there, the presenter should avoid merely reading.)

Milkshake Presentation II

Introduction

Good morning/afternoon. I've just come from a fast food restaurant, where I had the *worst* milkshake I've ever had and I *know* I make much better ones at home. So can you. I'll show you how.

Body

Ingredients:	ice cream
	vanilla
	Ovaltine
	milk

Equipment:	blender
	ice cream scoop or large spoon
	teaspoon
	tablespoon

Instructions: 6 scoops ice cream

1 teaspoon vanilla

2-3 tablespoons Ovaltine

milk to cover (about 1 pint)

3-4 short bursts. Blend 2 minutes.

Note: For audiences who are more familiar with the metric system, the measurements would be given as follows:

6 scoops ice cream

5 ml vanilla

30 to 45 ml Ovaltine

milk to cover (about half a litre)

3-4 short bursts. Blend 2 minutes.

Conclusion

(Review instructions ... then ...)

Well, it looks as if it's ready. Who'd like to be the first to try it?

The next step is to write the presentation on numbered cue cards. The information could be divided among three cards: one for the introduction, one for the ingredients and equipment, and one for the conclusion.

EXERCISE

■ **EXERCISE 4.2 DEMONSTRATION**

Each student will make a three-to-five-minute oral presentation. In these talks, you will show and explain either

1. how to do something, or

2. how something works.

Remember, you must demonstrate and talk to your audience at the same time. Writing on the board, showing pictures, or simply chatting with the audience is not a demonstration.

To prepare for your presentation, refer to your workbook and class notes.

Note: For future study, your demonstration will be videotaped as you present it to the class.

E X E R C I S E

■ EXERCISE 4.3   "UMS" AND "AHS"

When we can't think of what to say, we fill in the awful silences with "ums" and "ahs," or some other type of filler.

Instructions

1. Watch a videotape of yourself and your classmates in the first speech that you presented in class.

2. Record in the box below each filler when you first hear it. After you have heard a particular filler, start a count of how many times you hear it. The filler "you know" is provided as an example.

Filler	Number of times heard
you know	I I I I

As we can see, our everyday conversation is full of fillers. Pay attention to professional speakers such as radio and television announcers. These professional speakers are less likely to use fillers, but listen closely to their guests. You will probably notice the use of numerous fillers. Sometimes even the professionals stumble on their words, and *viola*—we hear the use of fillers!

How can you be cured of using fillers? If you are truly determined to eliminate or at least reduce your use of fillers, you must:

◆ Be aware of what fillers you are using.

◆ Watching a videotape of your presentations will tell you. Also, ask others—friends, family, fellow classmates.

◆ Realize how often the fillers are used.

◆ Each time you use a filler, have someone point it out until eventually the use will at least be reduced.

If you persevere, this method will work.

THE LAW ENFORCEMENT PRESENTATION

Constable Myra Hoi has just been detailed by her sergeant to prepare a presentation for the following week. The Seniors Against Crime Committee (SACC) has requested information about securing homes against theft.

P.C. Hoi is new to the Community Relations Unit and this will be her first presentation. She retrieves the notes from a special training seminar called "How To Conduct an Effective Presentation." She knows that "born speakers" are rare. Most people become good speakers with hard work. As she prepares for her presentation, she organizes the work that lies ahead into seven steps.

1. Analyzing the Audience

P.C. Hoi asks herself the following questions:

◆ What does my audience have in common?

◆ Is the audience made up of men or women, or both?

◆ How many people are in the audience?

◆ What is the average age?

◆ What is their background: education, religion, economic level, special interests?

◆ Why are they coming to listen to me?

◆ How much do they know already about the topic?

◆   What attitudes will they bring with them?

◆   What do I want to accomplish?

◆   What is my objective? Is it to teach, inform, inspire, motivate, persuade, debate, amuse, or to entertain? Or is it some combination of these?

■   EXERCISE 4.4   ANALYZING

Analyze P.C. Hoi's audience in this space.

E X E R C I S E

---

2. Selecting the Content of Your Presentation

P.C. Hoi knows that using a "shotgun approach," in which the speaker covers a large number of points but nothing is struck, simply doesn't work. The listener remembers little and suffers from "information over-load." P.C. Hoi's notes from the effective presentation course state:

◆ Focus and develop a few main ideas. Don't bury the audience in detail.

◆ Support each point by using devices such as the following: examples, analogies, quotations,* definitions, visuals, statistics, and stories. The audience should be able to relate to the support material.

* Quotations should be used sparingly. They should fit into the presentation, and should not be used just to sound impressive.

EXERCISE

■ EXERCISE 4.5   RECORDING IDEAS

Record a few main ideas for P.C. Hoi's presentation in the following space. Identify material to support each idea.

3. Organizing the Content

P.C. Hoi knows that she must design a structure that is easy to follow. As Ron Hoff says in his book *I Can See You Naked: A Fearless Guide to Making Great Presentations*:

> Your presentation structure, to be of any use whatsoever, must be simple enough to be remembered. It must be simple enough so that you'll remember what you want to say, and your audience will have no difficulty remembering what you told them.

Why is the organization of a presentation important? It allows the listener to concentrate solely on the information and not have to try to unravel the order of what you are saying. The most common organizational patterns are:

◆   chronological order, or order in time;

◆   spatial order, or space;

◆   problem–solution order;

◆   cause–effect order; and

◆   main idea–detail order.

■   **EXERCISE 4.6   ORGANIZING**

Organize P.C. Hoi's main ideas and supporting material in the following space.

EXERCISE

(Exercise 4.6 is continued on the next page.)

(Exercise 4.6 continued ...)

4. Overcoming Fear

People rate the fear of speaking in public as one of their greatest fears. The apprehension you may feel is normal. Try to make it work for you. Fear can energize you and motivate you to work harder to improve your presentation.

Fear can give you "an edge." Adrenaline becomes energy and your mind becomes more alert. New thoughts and ideas tend to emerge. P.C. Hoi remembers the first time she presented evidence in court. She was terrified of making a mistake and losing her case. She was also afraid of appearing foolish in front of the court. The defence lawyer intimidated her. As she was testifying, she remembered the warning from her fellow police officers about a philosophy allegedly held by some lawyers: "If you can't try the case, try the cop."

P.C. Hoi survived her first trial, and has become very good at providing evidence in court. Now she looks forward to being challenged by defence lawyers and judges when she appears in court. Her experience in testifying has improved her confidence in speaking publicly. However, every time she has to make a presentation or testify, she still experiences butterflies in her stomach. She offers some advice concerning reducing and controlling fear:

◆ Understand what it is you fear.

◆ Prepare and practise thoroughly. Much of what you fear is the fear of failure. Being prepared will lessen the possibility of failure and reduce your fear. Rehearse often and with a positive attitude.

◆ Gain experience. The more you speak in public, the more comfortable you feel. The positive experiences give you confidence and allow you to see the rewards of being a good speaker.

◆ Put your speaking experience in perspective. You do not have to present a flawless presentation. Be the best you can be and compete only with yourself.

◆ Move about and breathe deeply. Physical activity eases or lessens apprehension. Writing on the chalkboard or providing a demonstration allows you to use some excess energy. Likewise, using a visual aid provides some energy release, but it also takes the attention away from you. Don't plant yourself in one location.

◆ Don't look upon the audience as "a sea of faces." By scanning small pockets of people, it will seem as if you are doing what you do every day—talking to small groups of individuals.

◆ Develop an image of yourself as a successful, confident speaker and act like one. For example, stand tall and display good eye contact. Acting confident will actually increase your confidence.

5. Practising the Presentation

P.C. Hoi knows the benefits of rehearsing:

◆ You will know the material.

◆ Your mind will be less likely to go blank.

◆ You will feel more confident and less nervous.

◆ You can practise your use of voice (pause, pitch, variation, emphasis, speed, and volume).

◆ Your body language can reflect confidence.

Do not overpractise your speech until it does not sound natural or spontaneous. Know it well enough to give yourself confidence, but not to the point of memorizing it. Rehearse three to five times, then leave it and return to it later.

By videotaping your speech, you can view your performance and clearly see what areas need to be improved. Don't forget to stand while you practise and to incorporate your visuals into the presentation so that you are comfortable with them. By standing, you are more visible, you command more authority, your voice projects more, and you can gesture.

While practising your speech, time it. If it is too long, cut the content down or condense it. Do not speed up. You have been given a specific time-frame for your speech. Professionals always stay on time.

EXERCISE

■ EXERCISE 4.7   PRACTISING
Practise P.C. Hoi's presentation.

6. Delivering the Presentation

P.C. Hoi has three golden rules that she always follows when speaking publicly:

1. *Never read*   When reading a presentation:
   a. Your body language is restricted.
   b. You sound unnatural and insincere.
   c. You will never be a convincing speaker or develop self-confidence.

2. *Do not memorize*   When a presentation is memorized:
   a. It creates an invisible barrier and a lack of warmth.
   b. Your talk is mechanical, lacking enthusiasm and spontaneity. You tend to develop a monotone.
   c. Your credibility is questioned.
   d. Nerves may affect your memory and you may become lost.

3. *Eye contact is crucial*   Always look at the audience:
   a. Looking above the heads of the audience is obvious and makes the audience want to raise themselves the three or four inches necessary to meet your eyes.
   b. How will you know if the audience has stopped listening or is confused if you do not look at them?
   c. No matter how good your speech is, you will never be a good speaker or keep the attention of the audience if you do not look at them.

■ **EXERCISE 4.8　DELIVERING**

Deliver P.C. Hoi's presentation to the class.

E X E R C I S E

7. Controlling and Handling the Audience

Questions in larger groups need to be controlled because they may disrupt or even ruin your talk. On certain occasions as a police officer, you may be addressing a hostile, upset audience. Even placid audiences have to be controlled or you may find someone attempting to monopolize your attention and time. The person asking the question may be the only one interested in the answer. On the other hand, perhaps the answer to the question is coming in the presentation. Following are some suggestions for handling the audience:

◆　You can ask the audience to write questions on a piece of paper. The questions can then be asked during the question period at the end of the presentation.

◆　If you think a person is interrupting you for attention, be tactful and say something such as: "That's an interesting point. I'd like to speak privately with you at the end of the presentation to discuss it further." If the person is just seeking attention, it is highly unlikely that he or she will talk to you privately. After all, he or she is seeking the limelight in front of an audience.

◆　Sometimes a person will ramble on while asking a question. This can be handled by holding up your hand and asking politely: "What is the question?"

◆　On a rare occasion, you may be faced with an unruly individual or audience. If you feel that matters are getting out of control, you could call for a short break. The break will allow you to resolve the situation by dealing directly with the disruptive individual(s), or by notifying security, if necessary. An experienced speaker knows that he or she should not be the one to leave the room.

◆　Think carefully about questions you are asked before responding. A quick answer may end up being a poor answer.

◆　In some cases, it may be useful to restate the question to ensure that you have understood it.

◆　If you do not know the answer, don't bluff. Say that you will find out the answer and get back to the person.

◆　Don't embarrass the questioner.

◆　Don't drag your answer on.

Final Tips from Constable Hoi

◆ Cue cards containing key phrases may be used, but should not be heavily relied upon. (What if you drop them or find them in the incorrect order? Panic!) Don't write full sentences on the cards, or you may end up simply reading.

◆ Remember who your audience is. Tailor your language to suit the targeted group.

◆ Use conversational, simple language.

◆ Periodically summarize in case the listener has tuned out.

◆ Pause for a hushed effect, or to emphasize your next statement.

◆ If you leave something out during your speech, no one will know. If the information is crucial, then casually refer to wherever it belongs in relation to previously mentioned information. If you handle the situation smoothly, the audience will most likely not even realize that you have forgotten something.

NON-VERBAL COMMUNICATION DURING A PRESENTATION

Your body is a powerful instrument in your presentation. Words amount to only a portion of your message. How you say your message is actually more important than what you say.

Deportment

The impact of your message depends on your eye contact, body movements, gestures, facial expressions, voice, clothing, jewelry, makeup, and hairstyle, as well as your words. Every police officer knows the importance of "deportment." When you are interviewed for a police position, every interviewer is asking himself or herself: "How will this person look in a uniform?" Although a long, layered hairstyle may look great on a date, it probably won't look very professional or neat under a police hat. The same deportment rules apply when giving an oral presentation.

■ EXERCISE 4.9   AN OFFICER'S APPEARANCE

You have seen many officers in your life. Fill out the chart below, recording your observations of how you think police officers should look:

EXERCISE

Non-verbal language	Record how you think an officer should look
Eye contact	
Body movements	
Gestures	
Facial expressions	
Voice	
Clothing: consider uniform, and plain clothes if appearing in court or delivering a presentation	
Jewelry, for both females and males	
Hairstyle	
Makeup	

Eye Contact

The most important part of non-verbal communication in our culture is eye contact. As P.C. Hoi scans her audience of seniors, she is careful to look at the entire audience. Sometimes speakers will favour one side of the room, rarely looking anywhere else in the room. You may be tempted to focus on a few individuals in the audience. These people seem to be the ones with the friendly faces, not the grumpy person scowling from the back of the room. You must, however, force yourself to scan the room with your eye contact (including the grumpy individual), from one side of the room to the next, and from the back of the room to the front. A lack of eye contact makes the speaker appear distant, unconcerned, and less trustworthy. The speaker with poor eye contact loses touch with the audience and will not receive vital feedback from them. This feedback allows the speaker to adjust to the needs of the audience.

As P.C. Hoi looks around the room, she may notice a number of seniors turning their heads as if straining to hear. She may see a flurry of activity as a small group seem puzzled over something she has said. Clearly, the audience is giving a message to P.C. Hoi and she knows that she must now discover what the problem is. Had P.C. Hoi's eye contact been poor, she would not have been able to notice these important signals from the seniors.

Eye contact is a two-way street. It helps you read your audience's reaction to what you're saying. Your eyes also communicate to the audience your

◆ sincerity,

◆ interest in what you are saying, and

◆ confidence.

Facial Expressions

Facial expressions communicate emotions. The way that you feel will be displayed by your face. Police officers become very good at hiding their feelings. Check to see how you described the facial expression of potential police officers on the previous page. Though a neutral expression is appropriate on many occasions, do you think that P.C. Hoi will display it during her presentation to the seniors?

■ **EXERCISE 4.10   FACIAL EXPRESSIONS**

Describe what you think P.C. Hoi's facial expression would be like if she were talking to a group of Cubs or Brownies about street-proofing.

EXERCISE

Describe what facial expression she would have if she were addressing a group of youths from a tough inner-city school.

Posture

Posture is a large part of what the police call "deportment." During the delivery of her presentation, P.C. Hoi stands tall and appears confident. In fact, P.C. Hoi always stands this way, even if she is feeling tired, nervous, or frightened. She has learned through experience that her appearance is crucial; the public expect her to know exactly what she is doing and, although at times she may not be sure, her appearance does not give this away.

She has never forgotten that first week on the job, when she was the first officer on the scene of a four-car collision involving two fatalities. A citizen came running up to her, shouting to the large crowd of bystanders: "Thank Heavens, the police have arrived!" This was P.C. Hoi's first traffic investigation and she was terrified.

During her presentation to the group of senior citizens, P.C. Hoi avoids the following activities:

- leaning on the podium, desk, overhead, wall, or chalkboard;

- slouching;

- holding her body too tightly, an action that would make her appear weak; and

- hands in pockets—or worse, hands in pockets jingling change or keys.

   (The rules and regulations of most police services prohibit officers from placing their hands in their pockets while in uniform. Why do you think this rule exists?)

Gestures

Gestures are used to illustrate your messages. Effective body actions appear natural and are part of you and your presentations. The fact that some people gesture regularly, and some gesture rarely, shows that gestures are part of one's personality. Gestures, if used in excess, can be distracting; be careful that your gestures do not attract more attention than your presentation. Practised gestures appear insincere and unnatural; gestures should be comfortable and match what you are saying. During a presentation, avoid such gestures as:

- fixing your hair,

- adjusting your clothing,

- fidgeting with jewelry,

- clasping your hands in front of you or behind your back, and

- displaying repetitive, annoying habits.

   At times, if members of the public speak another language, or are deaf, or are very young or very old, P.C. Hoi relies heavily on gestures to communicate. Can you think of other instances when she would depend heavily on gestures?

Body Movement

Moving around a bit keeps the audience more alert and allows you to use your excess energy and to settle your nerves. Body movements emphasize transitions and the introduction of new information. Often an important point is made with a change in body position. However, three problems can occur. Body movement may be

◆ *Too much*   The audience wonders what the speaker will do next, paying more attention to the "dance" of the speaker than to the words of the speaker.

◆ *Too little*   The speaker appears afraid to move or just uninterested.

◆ *Patterned*   The speaker may not appear spontaneous and the audience becomes bored with the predictable, steady pattern.

Social Distance

The space between you and your listeners is often a crucial factor. Standing too close to an audience may make them feel uncomfortable. Standing too far away can give the impression that the speaker is uninvolved, uninterested, unapproachable, or uncomfortable. Sometimes objects, such as a large podium, can create distance and an unwanted barrier between the speaker and the audience.

Non-Verbal Language Before the Introduction and After the Conclusion

Your speech does not begin with the introduction, but actually starts as soon as the audience focuses on you as a speaker. Likewise, your speech does not end at the conclusion, but only after the audience has directed its focus away from you.

Before the Introduction

Show enthusiasm when you get up from your seat. Smile and walk to the speaking position with confidence, even though you may not feel confident. As you approach the front of the room, make sure that your body language is saying: I am worth listening to, and I am glad to be here.

Poor body language makes the audience feel uncomfortable. They expect the speaker to be confident, especially if that speaker is a police officer. If the speaker appears to lack confidence, they may not accept what the speaker is saying. They may not listen well and will quickly forget what was said. In court, it is crucial that the testimony of an officer not only be listened to, but that it also be accepted.

Before actually speaking:

◆ Stand in front of the audience with a sense of control.

◆ Establish eye contact with your audience, engage their attention, pause briefly, and then begin your speech.

After the Conclusion

After you have completed the conclusion, pause and then ask the audience if they have any questions or comments. Once the question period is over, walk (don't run) to your seat and sit down. Watch your non-verbal language and do not display the sense of relief that you are probably feeling. Remember, all eyes may still be on you.

Final Important Points and Review

An effective speaker needs to accomplish five tasks:

1. Make the listener want to learn more about the topic. People want to understand, and will remember information that they perceive as being relevant to their lives.

2. Communicate the information clearly in order to be understood. Do not overload the audience with information. "Information overload" can confuse the audience or cause them tune out. Unless absolutely necessary, do not use unfamiliar words or expressions.

3. Stress the main points. People learn by repetition, but be careful not to overdo it.

4. Find ways to involve the audience.

5. Look at the audience. Watch their faces to see how they are receiving your message and act accordingly. Likewise, pay attention to what their non-verbal language is telling you. Is it time to call a break or end your presentation?

An audience concentrates the most in the first 10 minutes, then at the end. Ideally, the maximum length of time for a presentation is only 20 minutes.

THE INTRODUCTION AND THE CONCLUSION

The introduction makes the first impression on the audience. The three main purposes of the introduction are to

1. gain the attention of the audience,

2. establish your qualifications or credibility, and

3. prepare the audience for the subject by opening their minds.

1. Gain the Attention of the Audience

Often the most important task in the introduction is to catch the audience's attention. If you fail to do this at the start, it is unlikely that they will listen to any of your presentation.

How do you capture their attention? This question will be answered with an example. Safety Officer Ewer Habid is visiting a high school classroom. The purpose of his talk is to

◆ inform the class of the dangers of impaired driving,

◆ persuade students to act responsibly, and

◆ dispel the "it will never happen to me" myth.

Described below are numerous techniques by which P.C. Habid could grab the attention of the class.

a. Startle the Audience with a Little-Known Fact

As he shows a chart on an overhead projector, P.C. Habid says:

> Perhaps you are not aware that 60 percent of fatalities are caused by impaired drivers.

b. Create Curiosity

P.C. Habid has brought with him a box covered with black wrapping paper. The students wonder what is inside the box. P.C. Habid allows each student to pick up a piece of paper from the box. The pieces of paper turn out to be death notices from the obituary section of a local newspaper. The death notices are about young people who have died as a result of the actions of impaired drivers.

c. Provide an Example

P.C. Habid selects three of these death notices. He gives a brief personal history of each victim. On a large screen, he shows slides of the victims as they grew up from babyhood. He tells the students that the victims' families want him to do this, in the hope that another young person will not drink and drive, or get into a vehicle with someone who is impaired.

d. Pose a Question

P.C. Habid knows that most people think that horrible accidents happen only to other people. He holds up an enlarged photograph of a fatal accident scene as he says:

> This is a photograph of a car. If I did not tell you what it was, you might never have guessed what the broken objects cluttering the roadway were. At one time, they were a 1999 Chevy Blazer. In that Chevy Blazer five high school students, who had been friends since grade 2, died because the driver of the car was impaired. Do you think that each one of those five young people woke up on the morning of the accident and thought: "What a beautiful spring day it is today. It's a good day to die"?

e. Use a Quotation

P.C. Habid tells the class:

> Many of you say that you would never drink and drive. Sometimes that's easier said than done. As Isaac Bashevis Singer said: "We know what a person thinks, not when he tells us what he thinks, but by his actions."

f. Tell a Story to Which the Listener Can Relate

The story can be either true or fictional. P.C. Habid tells the following story to the students:

> It's been a wonderful night dancing and drinking with your very best friends. Sarah has had way too much alcohol to drink, but who cares. She's young and she's happy. When it's time to go home, Sarah heads for the car. You try to stop her because you feel that she is drunk. Your friends tell you to mind your own business, that Sarah can handle it. She staggers out the door of the bar and that is the last time you ever see her alive. The next time you see her, she is resting in a coffin at a funeral home.

g. Use a Demonstration

P.C. Habid has brought to class a large display with a wheel. The students can rotate the wheel to see how many drinks they could consume before they would be legally impaired. The calculation varies according to sex and weight.

h. Genuinely Compliment the Audience

This method of catching attention is seen is many presentations. The danger of using this method lies in the fact that the audience may perceive the compliment as insincere. Bear this in mind if you plan to use it. P.C. Habid tells the students:

> I would like to thank you and Ms Zachara for inviting me here today. I can see that the class is eager to learn more about drinking and driving, or what we call impaired driving. Hopefully, a group of bright young people like you will learn from what I have to say.

i. Appeal to the Emotions of the Audience

All good speakers, especially politicians and advertisers, know that if you wish to change behaviour, you need to appeal to emotions. Touching a listener's emotions allows him or her to relate what you are saying to his or her own past experience. If you do not reach the emotions of an audience, you will probably not affect their behaviour.

Look at the examples previously listed in this section. What emotional appeals do they contain? P.C. Habid knows that if he wants to save any lives of students in the classroom, he's going to have to touch their emotions.

2. Establish Your Qualifications or Credibility

P.C. Habid states:

> I've been a member of the Traffic Division for six years. I've investigated 20 fatalities in that time period. Of the 20 deaths, 12 have been caused by an impaired driver. I've obtained criminal convictions in 8 of these cases. No charges were laid in the other 4 cases because the drivers were killed in the accidents.

(Notice that even here P.C. Habid is appealing to his audience's emotions.)

3. Prepare the Audience for the Subject by Opening Their Minds

This may include providing some background and a history of the problem so that the listener can understand the topic. Some terms may have to be defined or you may have to describe how you conducted your research. P.C. Habid tells the class:

> When Ms Zachara invited me to speak to you today, I decided to have each student complete a questionnaire before the session. Do you remember last week in guidance class when Ms Zachara asked you to write a quiz about how you spend your weekends? I have tabulated the results of the questions, and now I must sadly report to you that I believe that 20 percent of this class has a drinking problem.

When Do You Write the Introduction?

If you are already familiar with the topic, you may be able to write the introduction first; however, it is usually written once the research and the conclusion are completed. The introduction should include the purpose of the presentation as well as the central problem you are dealing with. Look at the previous sample techniques provided by P.C. Habid. What the officer is planning to cover in his presentation is clear from reading the introduction.

The Conclusion Is Your Final Opportunity

The conclusion is the final opportunity that you have to remind the listener of the purpose of your presentation. It is also the time to attempt to leave a memorable impression. The four main purposes of the conclusion are to

1. signal the audience that your oral presentation is about to end;

2. summarize the main points;

3. conclude the talk on a positive note; and

4. give recommendations, if appropriate.

The main points of the talk are rephrased and tied back to the purpose established in the introduction. The conclusion is the crux of the presentation and should be written in your own words. The conclusion may logically follow from the body of the presentation or may be reached after examining conflicting information. It should not, however, contain new ideas. The listener will consider your material and see how you arrived at your conclusion, though he or she may not necessarily agree with you. There is nothing wrong with this, however. Be objective in your conclusion and be prepared to defend yourself.

Many people feel that the conclusion is the most important part of the presentation. It should be to the point and clear, not filled with empty sentences, or a repetition of the introduction. No fluff!

Techniques That May Be Used in the Conclusion

a. Tell a Story

P.C. Habid tells the class:

> Michelle was just about to graduate from college. She wanted to own two dogs, join the OPP, get married, and have a family. Michelle didn't have a chance to do any of these things because of an impaired driver.

b. Make a Striking Statement

P.C. Habid reminds the class:

> Humans are funny beings. We never think tragic events will happen to us. My purpose for visiting your classroom has been to tell you that none of those dead young people we have talked about today ever thought that they would not see their 20th birthday. Not in their wildest dreams. Like you, they were going to have a long and happy life.

c. Ask a Question

P.C. Habid leaves the class with this question:

> Next time you, or a friend of yours, plan to drive a car following an evening of drinking, what are you going to do? Are you going to allow another statistic to be added to the grim stories I have told you about today?

d. Issue a Challenge

P.C. Habid continues:

> I suggest that each and every one of you will do the mature, responsible thing. Don't get behind the wheel. Don't allow your friend to drive. Don't become another statistic!

e. Compliment the Audience

P.C. Habid goes on to say:

> I can see as I look at your faces that you have taken my presentation today to heart. I can imagine you speaking up as you watch an intoxicated friend stumble toward his or her car, with car keys in hand. Above all, I can see you acting responsibly and living to a ripe old age … as you should.

f. Give a Quotation

P.C. Habid tells the class:

> From this day forward, I hope that you will show the responsibility that you owe yourself, your family, and the community. Impaired driving must be eliminated. The time has come to change dangerous behaviour that you may have shown in the past. As Oprah Winfrey said: "One of the great things about being young is that you can reject what came before, and you can change what lies ahead."

The techniques for the introduction and the conclusion can be used separately or in combination. In some of the conclusion examples, several methods are used together. As you can see, many of the same techniques are used for both the introduction and the conclusion. Partly, this is because the plan followed by many good speakers is, simply stated:

1. *Introduction*   Tell them what you're going to tell them.

2. *Body*   Tell them.

3. *Conclusion*   Tell them what you told them.

Question: What did P.C. Habid use in the sample introductions and conclusions to make a good presentation even better and more memorable?

Important Notes Concerning P.C. Habid's Presentation

The officer's language is conversational, clear, and easy to understand. A student with an A average could easily understand the officer's message, as could a student with a D average. Note that the officer's

◆   sentences are short,

◆   words are repeated at times,

◆   language is simple,

◆   ideas are clear and easy to understand, and

◆   sentences often begin with the main point of the sentence.

Words, however, usually account for only 7 percent of the speaker's effect on an audience. The most common mistake made by speakers is that they pay too much attention to their words. They think that words need to be very sophisticated and fancy. They do not know that how you say something is usually more important than what you say!

DID YOU KNOW ...

◆   7% of a speaker's effect on the audience is word choice

◆   55% of a speaker's effect on the audience is visual—that is, non-verbal

◆   38% of a speaker's effect on the audience is vocal—that is, varied and interesting

P.C. Habid, being an experienced speaker, knows that he must continually work on keeping his audience's interest. Numerous visual aids help, but he also makes sure that he involves the audience by:

◆   asking questions that need an answer,

◆   asking rhetorical questions (questions he does not expect anyone to answer),

◆   altering his voice level and speed,

◆   moving his body position and location (so that it does not appear as though he is "frozen" in one spot),

◆   doing something unexpected,

◆   asking the listeners to do something—for example, write on flip-chart paper,

◆   asking members of the audience to discuss a point with the people next to them, and

◆   asking the listeners to share—for example, "Has anyone ever experienced … ?"

Why Must P.C. Habid Offer Variety To Keep the Audience's Attention?

Your brain processes information over three times faster than a person can speak. The "free time" results in your thoughts wondering, and it is easy to become distracted and stop listening. Instead of listening to the speaker, you are admiring his or her suit, or criticizing his or her hair, or perhaps you are busy noting annoying mannerisms. Maybe you are formulating a question that you want to ask and are playing out in your mind what might happen during the interaction with the speaker.

There can be many others reasons why you are not listening, such as: the room is too hot or too cold, there are noisy distractions, you are hungry or tired, or the language being used by the speaker is over your head or too simple. You may even build a psychological barrier that prevents you from listening. This usually occurs when you strongly disagree with what the speaker is saying and you will not open your mind.

Studies indicate that you can generally listen for only 12 minutes, maximum, no matter how hard you try to listen! As you can see, there are many reasons why people do not listen. This is why speakers must offer variety to keep their listeners' attention.

ADVANTAGES AND DISADVANTAGES OF SPEAKING

Advantages	Disadvantages
The speaker can see the listener and respond appropriately	The listener cannot "re-listen" if he or she misses something
The speaker can slow down, speed up, repeat, and involve the listener	The writer often receives more attention
The speaker's body language and voice can add enthusiasm, emphasis, and emotion and keep the audience alert	The speaker must capture and hold attention of audience
The speaker can adjust language for audience, if necessary	

GUIDELINES FOR THE LISTENER

Listeners can do a great deal to help speakers with their fears:

◆ Positively reinforce the speaker with actions such as a nod, a pleasant smile, and an attentive appearance. Talking to a neighbour or reading is distracting to the speaker and may affect his or her confidence.

◆ Ask questions in a supportive way during the question period following the presentation. Ensure that your tone and manner do not make the speaker feel that he or she is being attacked.

◆ Do not focus on errors. If the speaker makes an error, do not draw attention to it by actions such as shaking your head, rolling your eyes, or using some other non-verbal method of communication to indicate that you have noticed the mistake. Pass over the error and continue listening. If it is really important to correct the error, you could do so politely during the question period, or speak to the presenter about it privately.

Constructive Criticism

The major purpose of constructive criticism is to improve one's public-speaking abilities. The presenter learns what he or she did well and what he or she needs to improve. When you offer constructive criticism of another, you are not claiming that you are a better speaker. You are offering your input to assist that person in future presentations.

Criticism is difficult to receive. After preparing for a long time and dealing with the anxiety surrounding your presentation, the last thing you want is to have others point out what you did wrong. Try not to personalize criticism—it can be an effective teaching and learning tool that will help improve your skills in public speaking.

Hints Concerning Giving Criticism

◆ *Be specific*   "I loved the speech. It was great!" does not say a lot.

◆ *Be objective*   Transcend you own biases.

◆ *Be positive and constructive*   Remember that your suggestions are for "the next presentation." Presentation style is hard to change (like a bad golf swing). It becomes ingrained and is part of a person's behaviour. By critiquing the speech now, you are not criticizing the past behaviour but offering suggestions for the future. Emphasize what is most important—that is, improvement for the next presentation.

◆ *Limit criticism*   You do not want to overwhelm the speaker, since your goal is to help him or her.

Hints Concerning Receiving Criticism

◆ *Accept the critic's point of view*   It may not be the same as yours but nevertheless deserves consideration.

◆ *Listen openly*   Because public speaking is so personal, one is tempted to block out criticism. If you do this, however, you may miss useful suggestions for improvement.

◆ *Respond without defensiveness*   Being defensive, as you try to protect your self-esteem, prevents effective communication and the possibility of learning from the experience. Remain calm and polite.

◆ *Separate speech criticism from personal criticism*   Although part of your speech has been criticized, your personality or your worth has not been. Try to see critical evaluation objectively.

◆ *Seek clarification for any criticism that you do not understand*   For example, if it is suggested that your voice was too weak, seek help on how to make it stronger. Try to understand the reasons for the criticism so that you can incorporate the suggestions into your next speaking experience.

REVIEW

An effective speaker needs to accomplish five tasks:

1. Make the listener want to learn more about the topic. People want to understand and will remember information that they perceive as being relevant to their lives.

2. Communicate the information clearly in order to be understood. Do not overload the audience with information. "Information overload" can confuse the audience or cause them to "tune out." Do not use unfamiliar words or expressions.

3. Stress the main points. People learn by repetition, but be careful not to overdo it.

4. Find ways to involve the audience.

5. Look at the audience. Watch their faces to see how they are receiving your message, and act accordingly. Likewise, pay attention to their non-verbal language. Bear in mind that an audience concentrates the most in the first 10 minutes, and then at the end. Try not to talk for more than 20 minutes.

VISUAL AIDS

Why Use Visual Aids?

◆ Seeing the message as well as hearing it results in better retention by the listeners.

◆ Some topics cannot be explained well without the use of visual aids.

◆ Visual aids tend to increase the attention span of the audience.

◆ Visual aids receive a favourable response from most audiences. The listener appreciates the effort made by the presenter.

General Guidelines for Using Visuals

Don't use visuals to improve a boring speech. Improve the speech first, and then use visuals to enhance it. Use audio and visual aids to support your ideas.

What is the most common visual aid? It's you! By your eyes and face and by the way you stand, walk, talk, and gesture, you convey your message visually to your audience.

Good visual aids have the following general characteristics:

1. *Simplicity*   Visuals should be portable, easy to manipulate, and easy to set up quickly.

2. *Clarity*   Visuals should increase understanding.

3. *Visibility*   The audience must be able to easily see and read the visuals.

How Do You Design Effective Visuals?

In a visual, pictures and/or cartoons are far better than words. If you are using words, limit them to labelling or identifying, reviewing, or summarizing. Letters should be at least ¾ in. (about 2 cm) high: the larger the better. The audience must be able to see the lettering.

Keep overheads simple. They should not contain too much information or be complicated. How many times have you seen a speaker use a visual aid with small type? Why does the speaker usually ask, "Can everyone see this?" when it is obvious that only the few front rows would be able to?

Tables rarely make good visuals because they are usually too small and too complicated. Pie and bar charts are fine to use because they are easy to understand. Charts and tables, on the other hand, must be explained. Never use a chart or table that you do not understand yourself.

Visuals can be used to catch attention in the introduction and conclusion, and to add humour, besides their usual use of explaining points.

EXERCISE

■ **EXERCISE 4.11   COMMON VISUAL AIDS ERRORS**

Complete the chart below.

Common mistakes	How could you correct the mistake?
Content requires the use of audiovisual aids, but they are not used	
"Overkill"—uses too many	
Improper handling	
Failure of equipment	
Equipment not available at site	
Visual aids too difficult to understand/read	

How To Avoid Visual Aids Problems

◆ Rehearse in advance.

◆ Check the equipment before the presentation. Does the facility have the equipment needed?

◆ Use objects that are easily portable.

◆ Use simple models.

◆ Use brief video and audio clips that create interest. No rule exists that says you must show the entire video.

Hints on Using Flip-Charts

◆ Stand to the right side if you are right-handed.

◆ Never write and speak at the same time.

◆ Face the audience when you speak. If you speak while you write, the audience will be watching the writing, not listening. Also, your voice will be muffled.

◆ Put down the marker or pen when it's not being used.

Hints on Using Overheads

◆ Do not turn on the overhead until the transparency is in place.

◆ Turn off the overhead before the transparency is removed.

◆ Allow the audience time to absorb the content.

◆ Show only what is relevant at the time. Cover the rest.

◆ Don't talk while the overhead is on, or allow time for the audience to take in the information before explaining it. Wait for the audience to turn their attention from the overhead to you.

◆ Explain the visual and the main point.

◆ Point to the transparency with a pen or pencil. Don't point to the screen.

◆ Don't look at the screen after you have checked that it is fine; look at the projector so that you do not turn your back (or the back of your head) to your audience.

◆ Don't walk between the projector and the screen.

◆ Remove the visual when it is no longer relevant.

◆ Turn the overhead off when it is not in use.

Advantages and Disadvantages of Visual Aids

Chalkboards

Advantages	Disadvantages
Reliable—nothing can break	Chalk is messy to use—can get on your clothing, or worse, your face
Quickly removed	Produces a teacher–student environment
Information can be easily added and taken away	Erased writing sometimes still visible
	Fixed object
	Suitable for small groups only
	Sound of chalk may be annoying
	Can audience at the back of the room see the writing?

Whiteboards

Advantages	Disadvantages
Same advantages as chalkboard, but cleaner	Fixed object
Pens add colour, and are visually more appealing than chalk	Suitable for small groups only
	Pens may run out, may be missing from room, or may be forgotten
	Smell may bother some people
	Sound of pen may be annoying

Flip-Charts

Advantages	Disadvantages
Easy to use	May be hard to write quickly yet keep writing legible
Easy to transport	Suitable only for small groups
	(Flip-chart advantages and disadvantages are continued on the next page.)

Many facilities have flip-charts	Not good for large amount of information
Flexible—can be prepared ahead of time or written on during the course of the talk	While writing, speaker's back is toward audience
Easy to add to for special effect	May run out of paper
	What do you do with previously written pages?

Overhead Projectors

Advantages	Disadvantages
Transparencies inexpensive and easy to create	Bulb may burn out and there may be no replacement bulbs
Flexible	Overhead may not be working properly
Order can be rearranged quickly if necessary	Fan noise can be distracting
Previous overhead can easily be referred to	After turned off, fan noise continues while unit is cooling
Screen easy to view	Must be constantly turned off or noise and bright light will take attention away from speaker
Possible to use with larger audiences	Speaker may forget to turn overhead off
Usually found in most organizations	Speaker's body may block view of screen
Most projectors are portable	Projector itself interferes with view of audience sitting nearby
With new technology, very impressive transparencies can be created	Inexperienced speakers fumble with overhead transparency because they often lay transparency down incorrectly
Information can be typed or photocopied so that it has a professional appearance	Speaker may face screen when reading information; overuse is annoying to audience

Computer-Generated Presentation

Advantages	Disadvantages
High visual impact	Possible incompatibility of equipment
Keeps attention of audience	Suitable equipment not available at site and transporting one's own is difficult
Listeners appreciate effort	Possible power disruption or failure
Many software programs produce handouts for audience	Possible insufficient power
	Speaker may focus on computer screen and not audience
	Lights may have to be turned off to see screen, with focus being taken away from speaker
	Difficult to write notes if lights must be off

Physical Objects

Advantages	Disadvantages
Can be easily seen, reducing need for verbal description	Passing around objects, papers, or displays interrupts the presentation and is distracting—attention is drawn away from the speaker
Audience does not distort image in their mind by misinterpreting description	Suitable for small groups only
Members of the audience can closely view after the presentation	If invited to view the object after the presentation, most of the audience will not do so

35mm Slides

Advantages	Disadvantages
Can display any image ever photographed or produced	Lights must be off and focus is taken away from speaker
Projectors owned by most organizations	Hard for audience to take notes
Can be shown to large audience	Cannot change order or omit slides without major interruption
Messages given can be powerful	Remote control may not work
Bright colours and clear images projected	If no remote control, need an assistant—otherwise speaker's focus is on operating equipment
	Equipment may malfunction and skip slides

Summary

Visual aids should be used to reinforce the presentation, not replace it. They are an integral part of your speech and serve important functions.

Always rehearse your speech and test your visual aids before using them. Can they be seen from all parts of the room? Is the information brief and can it be easily understood? Do you handle them correctly and with confidence?

Know your visuals inside out. Know:

◆ the order in which they will be presented,

◆ how you plan to introduce them, and

◆ what goes where and when.

EXERCISE

■ EXERCISE 4.12   ORAL PRESENTATION 1

P.C. Evans is scheduled to speak with a concerned citizens group about an increase in crime in their apartment complex. Four hours before the presentation, you are notified that P.C. Evans is ill. You are assigned the task, and as the most recent addition to the Community Policing Office, this is your first presentation.

You commence your preparation for the meeting. P.C. Evans has drafted a brief outline, but has not prepared a detailed speech.

(Exercise 4.12 is continued on the next page.)

(Exercise 4.12 continued ...)

You are horrified. Later, you find out from P.C. Evans that he never prepares a speech in full text, because he does not want to be tempted to make a crucial error that can occur in a speech—the error of reading. You wish you had known that before you went to the meeting.

Instructions

1. In the text that follows, read an imaginary account of what occurs.

2. In the text, underline and number 13 errors that you make.

3. At the end of the speech, in the chart provided, identify the type of errors that you have underlined and numbered. Correct the errors.

The outline seems a little simple, so you decide to improve it. You pack some slides that show security hardware that has been successfully used in the past to reduce crime in other apartments. You photocopy some charts and printouts of current statistics and convert them into an overhead. If you had the time, you would have enlarged them, but you tell yourself that it's better to have them as they are, rather than not to have them at all. You check the map to find the location of the meeting, and see that it is in a middle-class area of your division.

You arrive at the designated location 15 minutes early. As you drive up, you realize that the building is public housing. At this point you realize that the audience will not be filled with many members of the middle class.

The organizer greets you and takes you to the room where the meeting will be held. The only equipment in the room is a podium and an overhead projector. So much for the slides you brought!

As the room fills, you start to get a sinking feeling. Some of those attending are citizens with whom you have had contact. You wish that you hadn't changed P.C. Evans's simple outline.

The meeting has started. As you walk up to speak at the podium, you clear your voice and adjust your tunic. You wish that you had stopped at the dry cleaners to pick up a clean uniform that was better pressed. When you arrive at the podium, you grip it tightly and start the speech:

(Note: Your non-verbal language during the presentation is documented in italic type.)

(Exercise 4.12 is continued on the next page.)

(Exercise 4.12 continued ...)

I would like to take this opportunity to thank you for inviting me here today to provide you with an overview of multiple methods of securing your building and its environs from crime-encouraging signals.

First off, I would like to apologize for appearing somewhat disorganized and disoriented. You see, my partner, Constable Evans, was supposed to be here tonight, but due to illness I was designated by my superiors to attend. I hope that you will bear with me.

You are gripping the podium so tightly that your knuckles are white. As you quickly glance up between reading sentences, you see some confused faces sprinkled with some unfriendly faces. You decide it is better to keep your head down so that the faces do not distract you.

As you proceed through the speech, you stay still in a fixed position at the podium. About 10 minutes into the presentation, you notice that somehow you have acquired a pen, which you are stabbing into the air as you make your points. You continue with various suggestions for the group about how to reduce crime in the building.

I have mentioned previously the importance of illumination for the reduction of crime. By installing XPSA extra-illumination devices, your mischief occurrences should diminish to the potential point of elimination. The XPSAs can be purchased at your local commercial distributor for about $100. That's not a bad price for peace of mind.

The presentation continues for 20 more minutes in the above manner, with you providing information about the latest computer hardware that has been shown to reduce crime. You throw some detailed charts and flow charts with the latest statistics on to the overhead projector. Finally, during the conclusion, you look up at the crowd and discover that about a quarter of the original audience seems to be missing. Other members appear to be confused, while a few are visibly angry. You decide to forget about having a question period. As you are about to sit down, several hands are raised to ask questions. A woman asks: "So far you have suggested that we buy about $500 worth of this computer hardware to make our lives better around here. If my monthly income before I pay rent is only $700 a month, where the @#%* am I supposed to find $500?" Another question follows from an elderly man: "What is an extra-illumination device?"

(Exercise 4.12 is continued on the next page.)

(Exercise 4.12 continued ...)

> After this question, a loud buzz fills the room as the audience agrees with the old man. You hear questions such as the following being yelled out: "Why don't you talk English?" and "What the heck are you talking about?" along with "We pay our taxes for the police to protect us, not for the police to come to our apartment to tell us how to spend money. I bet the police are getting a kick-back from the store that sells all that stuff."
>
> The organizer of the meeting abruptly stands up, thanks you very much for coming, and calls a quick end to the meeting. You are rapidly ushered out the rear door. As you drive back to the station you ask yourself: "What went so terribly wrong?"

Identify the types of errors that you have underlined and numbered. Correct the errors.

Errors	Corrections
1.	
2.	
3.	
4.	
5.	

(Exercise 4.12 is continued on the next page.)

(Exercise 4.12 continued ...)

Errors	Corrections
6.	
7.	
8.	
9.	
10.	
11.	
12.	
13.	

■ **EXERCISE 4.13   ORAL PRESENTATION 2**

E X E R C I S E

Introduction

This exercise

◆   is a review of the content of this chapter on oral presentation,

◆   helps develop your skills in creating and effectively using visual aids, and

◆   provides you with an opportunity to offer constructive criticism.

Instructions

1.   In groups, create a two-minute group presentation about "street-proofing." Imagine that you have been asked to speak about this topic to a particular audience. Each group has a distinctive audience and objective. Likewise, each group has a different visual aid that will be used to enhance the presentation. Use the following chart to discover your group's particular audience or listener, objective, and visual.

Groups	Audience/listener	Objective	Visual
1 & 2	A public school grade 3 class from an upper-middle-class suburb	To inform	Chalkboard
3 & 4	A public school grade 3 class from an inner-city school in a downtown core; most students live with families who are anti-police	To inform To persuade	Overhead
5 & 6	A group of business people from the Rotary Club, who may donate some funds to your street-proofing organization if you can convince them that your cause is worthy	To inform To persuade	Flip-chart paper
7 & 8	A group of concerned parents who are members of a local church group	To inform	Physical object

Note: Two examples of each (audience/listener, objective, and visual) are provided for comparison purposes.

2.   After your group has presented, work together as a group to summarize to the class positive and negative aspects of using the particular visual aid you were assigned. The visual aids

(Exercise 4.13 is continued on the next page.)

(Exercise 4.13 continued ...)

section of this chapter, beginning on page 112, will give you some ideas.

3. Constructively critique the presentations. For the duration of each presentation, the class will become the target audience. For example, for groups 1 and 2, the class will become an upper-middle-class group of grade 3 students from the suburbs. Put yourself in the place of the audience and judge the effectiveness of the presentation. As a listener, don't forget to

 ◆ actively listen,

 ◆ ensure that your body language is positive and indicates interest in the presentation,

 ◆ keep an open mind, and

 ◆ listen for unsound arguments, generalities, or untruths.

Prepare to provide constructive feedback at the end of each presentation. The class may be divided into quarters, with each section concentrating on a particular aspect of the presentation.

¼ of the class	¼ of the class	¼ of the class	¼ of the class
Comment on group's introduction and conclusion	Comment on group's eye contact, voice, posture, and other non-verbal language	Comment on message sent, content of presentation; was the objective met?	Comment on quality of visual and effectiveness of use

■ **EXERCISE 4.14   ORAL PRESENTATION REVIEW**

E X E R C I S E

1. Why study public speaking?

2. Why can an audience only listen for approximately 12 minutes?

3. List techniques that a speaker may use to keep an audience listening.

(Exercise 4.14 is continued on the next page.)

(Exercise 4.14 continued ...)

4. Why is listening sometimes referred to as "the forgotten skill"?

5. What is the most common mistake made by inexperienced speakers?

6. Why should a presenter speak in a conversational, simple manner, and not in a fancy, sophisticated manner?

(Exercise 4.14 is continued on the next page.)

(Exercise 4.14 continued ...)

7. List the advantages that a speaker has over a writer. List the disadvantages.

8. How should a person go about starting to prepare a speech?

9. When asked to speak as a guest, what do you need to know before you start your preparation?

(Exercise 4.14 is continued on the next page.)

(Exercise 4.14 continued ...)

10. In general, how many main points should you have in your presentation, and why?

11. Make a list of what happens if a speech is read.

12. Make a list of what happens if a speech is memorized.

(Exercise 4.14 is continued on the next page.)

(Exercise 4.14 continued ...)

13. You are making a presentation about drug abuse to a high school class. You intended not to read from your cue cards. However, when you start the presentation, you realize that, even though you know the material, you are simply reading from the cue cards. Your nervousness keeps your eyes down on the cue cards. How could this have been avoided?

14. List other problems that can result from using cue cards.

(Exercise 4.14 is continued on the next page.)

(Exercise 4.14 continued ...)

15. Fill in the following chart, describing what your body should be saying during your presentation.

Aspect of body language	Details of what your body should be saying
Eyes, facial expression	
Body movements	
Posture	
Clothing, jewelry, hairstyle, makeup	
Gestures	
Voice	
Handling lecterns or other barriers affecting space / distance from audience	
Body language as you approach the front of the room to deliver the presentation	
Body language as you step away after delivering the presentation	

(Exercise 4.14 is continued on the next page.)

(Exercise 4.14 continued ...)

16. Describe the benefits of practising your presentation.

17. What should you do if you realize during the speech that you have forgotten a portion of it?

18. How does an audience react to poor body language?

(Exercise 4.14 is continued on the next page.)

(Exercise 4.14 continued ...)

19. Describe how a presentation should be practised.

20. Why must questions from an audience be controlled?

21. How could you control an individual asking a "rambling" question?

(Exercise 4.14 is continued on the next page.)

(Exercise 4.14 continued ...)

22. True or false?

    a. Every effort should be made by
       the speaker to eliminate nervous
       energy.   **TRUE**   **FALSE**

    b. A person is either a "born speaker"
       or not.   **TRUE**   **FALSE**

23. What have you learned about public speaking from this
    chapter that you did not know before?

CHAPTER 5
Report Writing

INTRODUCTION TO REPORT WRITING

Memo books and report writing go hand in hand. Details recorded in a memo book provide the information needed to write a report. Therefore, it would be beneficial to study this chapter and the next one together.

Imagine yourself at a serious crime scene, where you have to

◆ restore order,

◆ administer first aid,

◆ locate weapons,

◆ apprehend a suspect(s),

◆ locate witnesses and victim(s),

◆ separate witnesses,

◆ obtain and broadcast full descriptions and information from witnesses,

◆ order and assist ambulance and fire department crews,

◆ notify specialized units and supervisors to attend the scene,

◆ control the public and the media, and

◆ protect the crime scene.

An officer has a lot of duties at a crime scene. The last thing you may be thinking about is writing a record in your memo book, which, in turn, will become the basis of the reports to be written later. Compared with the activities listed above, report writing may seem insignificant, but ultimately your success in obtaining a conviction in court may rest on your record-keeping and report-writing skills.

The Importance of Writing a Good Police Report

1. *An error in your report can affect your testimony in court*   You can be embarrassed trying to explain errors in your report while providing testimony in court. Not only does it cloud your reputation, but it reflects poorly on your service and fellow police officers. Once embarrassed and confused, you may forget important information, contradict yourself, appear hesitant, and make a poor impression overall on the jury and the court. If you become angry because of

your mistake, you may easily become goaded into more errors, such as losing your temper with the defence counsel.

If an officer's testimony can be discredited, it creates an illusion of incompetence. In the witness box, officers are vulnerable, and a simple spelling error in a report may easily result in the defence questioning your abilities.

Even on a guilty plea, the sentence imposed may be influenced by your report. The judge may base his or her decision on your report.

2. *Without a good report, the Crown cannot do his or her job*   Usually, most of the information that the Crown attorney receives comes from your report. The Crown may even decide whether to proceed to trial, or to plea bargain, depending on your report. If your report is poor, the Crown may decide not to place you on the stand, for fear of the outcome.

Crowns have heavy case loads, and usually do not meet with you before the trial. More often than not, the Crown is looking at the case envelope for the first time just a few minutes before the case comes before the judge. The report must be clear, well written, complete, compact, and easy to follow, so that the Crown is able to proceed.

3. *Followup reports may prove difficult if a report is poor*   Followup reports by other officers and/or specialized units depend on clear, accurate reports. An ineffective report may be useless, placed aside temporarily, or have to be reinvestigated.

Most followup reports are carried out by plainclothes officers and specific units. If you earn the reputation of being a poor report writer, you will most likely never be considered for an opening in any of these units. Officers who work in these units may never have met you, but they may groan when a report written by you appears on their desk!

4. *Reports should reflect a professional image*   Reports are read by your supervisors, other government agencies, lawyers, judges, jurors, insurance companies, the media, and the public. They must show competence and credibility.

Reports are also used for statistics and published documents. If information is missing, the report may become meaningless. Accurate information in a report could mean an engineering change in a poorly designed traffic intersection, more money for part of the police budget, or new equipment for the rank and file.

5. *Reports affect your career*   Good report-writing skills are used to measure competency for lateral transfers and/or promotions. If you work for a large service, high-ranking officers may not know you personally, but they will have formed an opinion of you on the basis of your reports.

6. *Poor reports affect the safety of fellow police officers* Information from reports keeps fellow workers informed. Details entered into computers must be accurate. Enforcement work can be hazardous, and any information, no matter how small, may help. For example:

◆ If you input the wrong licence plate information of a stolen vehicle and an unsuspecting officer pulls that vehicle over, then you have placed that officer in a dangerous situation.

◆ If you file a missing person report about an escapee from a hospital, your report must include the missing person's mental condition, psychiatric problems, and any other information concerning potential danger.

◆ As you carry out your daily duties, you deal with a wide range of humanity. When you deal with these individuals, you rely heavily on Canadian Police Information Centre (CPIC) information to warn you of any potential threat to your safety. If vital information is missing, you may suffer the consequences.

The Four Steps in Report Writing

The four steps in report writing are:

1. to gather facts,

2. to record those facts in your memo book,

3. to organize the facts, and

4. to write the report.

A report tells what happened, explained in a simple, clear, and precise manner. It is "just the facts." If hearsay, inferences, or opinions appear in a report, they must be identified as such. The reader of the report must be able to understand what happened. Never make the reader guess. A report also tells what actions the police took.

It is important to be able to determine the facts. Facts are firsthand knowledge of something; they can be verified. Facts must be correct. Examples of facts include:

◆ physical evidence;

◆ investigative actions—for example, what actions you took; and

◆ statements that you wrote (although the statement you recorded may be hearsay and inference, the fact remains that you took it.)

When writing a report, you must separate facts from hearsay, inferences, and opinions. See the following chart.

Term	Definition	Example	Explanation
Facts	Firsthand knowledge/ experience.	"P.C. Wynnyk observed a red Toyota Celica drive away."	P.C. Wynnyk sees the red Toyota Celica drive away. She recognizes the make and model because she is familiar with all makes and models of vehicles.
Hearsay	Information given to you by other sources, such as victims, suspects, and witnesses.	"The complainant reported that she observed a red Toyota Celica drive away."	The complainant may be mistaken. The phrase "The complainant reported" tells the reader that it is not a verified fact that the vehicle is a red Toyota Celica.
Inferences	Things that you infer or draw from something you have seen or experienced. Such conclusions are based on what you observed or were told.	"Based on the statements of the four witnesses, it appears that a red Toyota Celica drove away."	After speaking to four witnesses (whom you believe to be reputable), you infer, or draw the conclusion, that the car is a red Toyota Celica and that it drove away. The inference is identified in the report by these words: "it appears that …"
Opinions	Opinions are what a person thinks about something or someone. Opinions can sometimes be biased judgments.	"The hot and fancy red Toyota Celica drove away."	Judgments have no place in a report. In this example, the biased judgment that the Celica is "hot and fancy" is irrelevant. Usually, opinions are not part of a police report. If an opinion is proven to be a fact, then it is no longer an opinion and appears in a report as a fact. Generally speaking, opinions are not allowed in court during testimony. There are some exceptions. If an opinion is placed in a report, it is usually limited to the writer's estimation of the credibility of a witness or an informant. Opinions are usually introduced by the phrase, "It is the opinion of the writer … ."

GUIDELINES FOR GOOD REPORT WRITING

1. Be accurate. Use your five senses: seeing, hearing, feeling, smelling, and tasting. Answer "the 5 W's"—who, when, where, what, and sometimes why.

    Look at the relationship of each "W" to the appropriate information. For example, when you ask "Who?" do you mean:

    ◆ Who is the victim?

    ◆ Who is the subject?

    ◆ Who is the suspect?

    ◆ Who is the witness?

    ◆ Who is the owner of the property?

    ◆ Who is the complainant?

    ◆ Who found the property?

    ◆ Who owned the car?

    ◆ Who drove the car?

    ◆ Who is the officer at the scene?

    ◆ Who is the supervisor?

    ◆ Who are the other persons at the scene?

    ◆ Who are the other investigators (for example, sexual assault squad, emergency response unit)?

    ◆ Who are the other agencies (for example, Children's Aid Society, VICARS)?

    In other words, depending on the facts of the case, the 5 W's can be applied an unlimited number of times.

2. Be impartial. You must be unbiased and open-minded, basing any inferences only on facts. Use objective language. Leave out judgments.

3. Keep your sentences short. If your sentences are too long, information becomes confusing or obscured. Using short sentences also reduces the chance of grammatical errors.

4. As much as possible, begin each sentence with the subject of the verb. This helps makes the sentence straightforward.

5. Reports are written in the third-person impersonal—for example, "the investigating officer," "P.C. Ollie," and "the writer." If P.C. Ollie wrote the report, he refers to himself in the terms mentioned above, not as "I." The third person is used in an attempt to show objectivity.

6. Keep pronoun references clear. Pronouns refer to the closest noun. If a pronoun is repeated, or there is more than one noun in a sentence, then it is hard to tell which noun the pronoun is replacing. For example: "Ali and Jeremy were arrested. He was very upset by the incident." (Who is "he"—Ali or Jeremy?)

7. Use active verbs, not passive verbs. The verb should describe the action of the subject, rather than something happening to the subject. For example, write: "The man robbed the female victim." Do not write: "The female victim was robbed by the man."

8. In general, use the past tenses of verbs.

9. Do not use uncommon abbreviations or slang.

10. Use diagrams for complex descriptions.

11. Keep paragraphs short, with one point per paragraph. This makes it easier to find specific information. The maximum number of sentences per paragraph should be six.

12. The report should be organized in chronological order, as you experienced the event, or in the order in which the event unfolded.

13. Handwritten reports must be legible.

14. Use supplementary report forms for detailed information that would interrupt the flow of the incident. Any details that do not add to the understanding of the report may be placed on a separate supplementary report. For example: "A quantity of jewelry, cash, and liquor were stolen at the Break and Enter. See supplementary report for complete description of stolen property."

15. Make sure that there are no spelling errors.

16. Record a description of the scene. For example: residence, commercial, type of building, types of doors, windows, locks, alarm systems, point of entry, point of exit, appearance of rooms, and physical evidence.

17. Record all persons at the scene, such as all police personnel (constables, supervisors, detectives, specialized units); ambulance staff and unit number(s); firefighters and pumper number(s); civilians; and other agencies.

18. On a record of arrest, describe how the suspect was arrested. Was force applied? Record all injuries and how they were sustained, if known. Record the times at which the suspect's rights were read and when the suspect was cautioned, if cautioned.

19. Be brief, yet complete. All essential information must be included, whereas irrelevant information must be omitted. Be brief by excluding unnecessary information. The boxed areas of each report contain a wide range of information, none of which needs to be

repeated in the "details of the offence" section (in effect, the body or story) of the report. For example, the boxed area of an arrest report contains about 20 pieces of information concerning the accused. None of these details has to be included in the details of the offence section. The writer simply records "the accused" when making reference to the person charged.

What Is Included in a Police Report Description?

W   *What* are you describing? Kind of article—for example, watch, gun, bicycle, motor vehicle, purse, jewelry.

A   *Appearance*: colour, size, shape, design, calibre, length of barrel, finish. Condition: age, state of repair, date of purchase, dirty, clean, appears new, shabby. Material: gold, silver, metal, wood, glass, leather. Accessories.

N   *Number* of items.

T   *Type*, make, model, style, manufacturer's name, trade name.

E   *Extraordinary* features that make the item unique, unusual, or identifiable. Serial number; engraving; initials; unusual marks caused by wear.

D   *Dollars*. What is the value? Is it insured?

FACTS IN ISSUE

When gathering information to record in your memo book, the facts in issue (or the elements of the offence) must be considered. The information written in your memo book is used to write your report(s). This information is ultimately presented in a court of law. The importance of good record-keeping and report-writing skills is obvious.

The facts in issue are the ingredients of the crime; they are the facts that must be proven beyond a reasonable doubt to establish guilt. Let's compare the conviction of an accused with the baking of a cake. In order to successfully achieve the desired outcome, certain elements must be included. Simply stated, a solid case in court must be presented to obtain a conviction, and the proper ingredients must be used to create a pleasing cake.

When making a cake, every essential ingredient must be carefully measured and added to the mixing bowl. If a necessary ingredient is lacking, the cake will not successfully rise and/or taste the way it was intended to taste. Lacking just one necessary ingredient will result in failure. The same is true of a court case.

When building a *prima facie* case, all the facts in issue must be proved beyond a reasonable doubt, or else the case is weakened. It may slump and fall, like the cake. If this occurs, then guilt is not established beyond a reasonable doubt. In the Canadian court system, if this occurs, the law states that the accused must be let go.

Sometimes the analogy of a bridge is used to explain the facts in issue. Each one of the columns supporting the bridge can be considered a fact in issue. If the evidence in one column is weak, then that part of the bridge will fall down and the bridge will collapse. The accused will not be convicted. It is the job of the defence to weaken any supporting column of evidence built by the Crown. Through cross-examination, or through the presentation of contradictory evidence, the defence can create a doubt about the supporting evidence.

In criminal court, "the burden of proof is on the Crown attorney to establish a *prima facie* case." These words mean that the Crown attorney, who represents society's interests, must prove the case against the charged person beyond a reasonable doubt. The Crown establishes a *prima facie* case (a "solid case") by establishing the facts in issue, also known as the elements of the offence.

Every offence requires that certain general facts in issue be proved. They include such facts as:

1. *Who* identity of the accused;

2. *When* date, time;

3. *Where* location of the offence; and

4. *What* the specific ingredients of the offence.

To discover the specific facts in issue that must be proved for an offence, the statute itself and perhaps case law must be referred to.

As previously mentioned, the burden of proof is on the Crown attorney to establish a solid case. Once the Crown establishes the facts in issue, the burden switches to the defence to create a reasonable doubt about the case. If the defence attorney does not feel that the Crown has established a *prima facie* case, then he or she will ask the judge to dismiss the charge. If the judge accepts the defence's argument, then the charge is dismissed and the accused is free to go. There is no need for the defence to provide evidence to contradict the Crown, because the Crown has not established a *prima facie* case. If the judge disagrees with the defence, then he or she will order the trial to continue.

Let's use a simple example of speeding 90 km/h in a 50 km/h zone to help us understand the facts in issue. The key question is: "What do you need to prove this case beyond a reasonable doubt?"

Note: A speeding offence, under the *Highway Traffic Act* (HTA), is not a criminal offence; it is an offence against a provincial statute. In traffic court, the presiding judicial official is a justice of the peace (JP). In court, the JP is called "Your Worship."

Facts in issue	Details establishing facts in issue/elements of the offence (example of part of the testimony an officer may provide)
1. *Who*	"The driver identified himself with a valid Ontario driver's licence as Matt Smith, DOB 23 March 1980, of 18 Park St. in Sudbury, Ontario. The picture on the driver's licence matched his appearance."
2. *When*	"On Tuesday, November 30, 1999, at approximately 2:38 p.m., I observed a white Volkswagen Beetle, licence JJE 337 travelling …"
3. *Where*	"… eastbound on Lakeshore Blvd. East, at Yonge St. in the city of Toronto, in the fast lane …"
4. *What* Specific facts in issue needed to prove a speeding charge	The radar clocked the speed of the Beetle at 90 km/h in a posted 50 km/h zone. Signs were clearly posted. The radar equipment was functioning properly at the time of the offence. The radar equipment had been tested at that location for interference and it was functioning properly. The officer issuing the ticket had been trained to operate the radar equipment. The location of the officer and the radar equipment at the time of the offence. The weather and road conditions.

■ EXERCISE 5.1   LISTING FACTS IN ISSUE

Look at the facts in issue listed in the preceding chart. Record the facts in issue that you think would have to be proven in any court case.

EXERCISE

EXERCISE

■ EXERCISE 5.2 RECORDING FACTS SPECIFIC TO A CHARGE

Record the facts that are specific to a charge of speeding.

Facts in Issue Example: Trespass at Night

Everyone who, without lawful excuse, the proof of which lies on him, loiters or prowls at night on the property of another person near a dwelling-house situated on that property is guilty of an offence punishable on summary conviction. (*Criminal Code*, RSC 1985, c. C-46, s. 177)

General Facts in Issue

(These are always the same.)

1. *Who* did it

2. *When* it was done

3. *Where* it was done

Specific Facts in Issue

(The specific ingredients of the offence. These must be determined from reading the appropriate section in the *Criminal Code*.)

4. *What*

   ◆ without lawful excuse,

   ◆ loiters or prowls,

◆ at night, and

◆ on the property of another near a dwelling-house on that property.

■ EXERCISE 5.3   ASSAULT VIDEO

1. Watch a video of an assault.

2. Locate the assault section in the *Criminal Code*.

3. Write in your memo book the details of the event. Keep in mind the facts in issue that must be proved beyond a reasonable doubt in order to establish a *prima facie* case.

4. Write an assault report in the blank general occurrence report supplied, page 173.

EXERCISE

■ EXERCISE 5.4   CREATING A VIDEO

In groups of four:

1. Choose a section of the *Criminal Code*.

2. Identify the facts in issue that need to be proved beyond a reasonable doubt in order to establish a *prima facie* case.

3. Create and videotape a brief scenario surrounding this offence.

4. Present the videotape to the class. Ask the class to identify the facts in issue.

5. Lead the class toward the solution.

EXERCISE

■ EXERCISE 5.5   DESCRIPTION

1. Select a member of the class as your subject. Do not tell anyone whom you have chosen.

2. In your memo book, write a complete description of your subject.

3. Read your description to the class without naming your subject.

4. Assess the accuracy of your description by how long it takes the class to identify your subject.

EXERCISE

REPORT WRITING: DETAILS OF THE OFFENCE SECTION

The "details of the offence" or "synopsis of the offence" (or whatever it may be called) section of a report is the narrative, or the story of what happened. If you run out of room in the details of the offence section, then you can finish the narrative on a supplementary report.

The narrative always follows a certain expected pattern of chronological order. Everyone involved in the legal process expects this of your report.

Reports of all officers look and sound alike. Your supervisors expect that your reports will be the same as all other officers' reports. The narrative must be predictable for all parties involved in the legal system.

When you testify in court, the Crown attorney, the defence attorney, and the judge will all expect you to tell your story in the same way in which other officers testify. Your testimony follows the details of what you have written in your report. The notes in your memo book, which you take to the stand with you, will correspond to your report. (You cannot use your memo book in court unless you receive permission from the judge or justice of the peace. See page 201 in chapter 6, "Memo Books," for the process followed to obtain permission.)

The Crown has your report in front of him or her as the court case proceeds. If a guilty plea is recorded, then the Crown will read out the "details of the offence" section of your report. If your report fails to establish the facts in issue, then the defence lawyer will call for a dismissal of the charge. If the defence lawyer does not notice the flaw in the report, then the judge will most likely dismiss the charges. Remember, it is the judge's job to be impartial and to ensure that the accused receives a fair trial.

Report writing in the enforcement field is different from report writing in other professions. It is the opposite of résumé writing. In a résumé, no short forms are used because they may indicate negative things about you—for example, that you

◆ are lazy and can't be bothered,

◆ don't care enough to put forth your best effort,

◆ lack professionalism, or

◆ settle for second best.

In report writing, on the other hand, short forms are accepted and expected.

Examples of Short Forms and Their Uses

a/m time and date	Some police services accept this as a short form for "above-mentioned time and date." This phrase refers to the time(s) and dates recorded in the boxed area above the "details of the offence."
DOB	date of birth

W/B, E/B, N/B, S/B	westbound, eastbound, northbound, southbound
AKA	also known as
approx	approximately
POE	point of entry
PI	personal injury accident
PD	property damage accident
SOCO	scenes of crime officer

If short forms are used, the narrative may seem to be lacking information, but it really isn't. The reader simply has to refer to the boxed information area above the "details of the offence" section to locate the information. For example: "The complainant reports that between the a/m times and dates her home was broken into."

In the boxed area of the report, the reader sees the full name of the complainant. All pertinent details about the complainant are available in the boxes that follow the complainant's name. Pertinent details include: the complainant's full address with postal code, home and business telephone numbers, the complainant's DOB, and the complainant's relationship to the suspect (if any).

The a/m times and dates are meaningless until you look at the boxed area above the narrative. There, you discover that sometime between 17:30 on Friday, July 2 and 18:00 on Sunday, July 4 the complainant's home was broken into. In this example, the complainant locked up her house on Friday, July 2 at 17:30, and returned home from the cottage on Sunday, July 4 at 18:00, only to discover the break and enter.

If the crime occurs on one day, the phrase would be: "between the a/m times on the a/m date." If a witness or the victim knows the time, what would the phrase be?

Special Boxed Area Notes

◆ The date of birth is usually written "day   month (in alpha)   year." Writing "03 Apr. 80" is clear. Writing "03/04/80" is not clear, since it could be Mar. 04 80.

◆ Addresses, with postal codes, must be written in full.

◆ Business telephone numbers allow followup investigators to contact people during the day.

◆ Many different types of reports are written on the general occurrence form. Some of the boxes may not be relevant to the occurrence and would be left blank. For example, if a report were about a missing purse, then the boxed areas concerning a vehicle would be left blank.

You should always obtain DOBs of all participants and/or witnesses in any occurrence. Why should you? All persons should be checked on CPIC in the event that they are wanted or considered dangerous. CPIC provides you with other reliable information, such as if certain persons are currently before the courts and on what charges. If CPIC tells you that a particular individual is wanted on a warrant, the law states that the information from CPIC constitutes reasonable grounds for an arrest. If a warrant is outstanding, however, pay attention to the radius for return to the police service who issued the warrant. If the warrant is only province-wide and was issued in British Columbia, then there are no grounds to arrest that person with whom you have come in contact in Ontario.

In a record of arrest report, the boxed area includes information about the accused, similar to that about the complainant. In fact, there are significantly more details, such as a complete physical description. In the narrative, however, you cannot simply say "the accused" as you can "the complainant." In court it is crucial to establish the identify of the accused. It is a basic "fact in issue," or "element of the offence," that must be established beyond a reasonable doubt in order to obtain a conviction.

In the narrative section of a record of arrest report, you must clearly identify the accused. Remember, if there is a guilty plea, there is no trial. The Crown reads your record of arrest in court, word for word. If you have not identified the suspect to the satisfaction of the court, your case is lost. For example: "The accused identified herself with a valid Ontario driver's licence as Karen Singh, DOB 03 Mar. 74, of 51 Main St. in Sudbury, Ontario."

In court, while providing testimony at the trial, you repeat this same information while pointing at the accused. If the Crown attorney or the judge does not clearly see you point, you will be asked by one of them: "Do you see that person before the court today?"

You would answer, "Yes," and point to the accused, perhaps adding: "She is sitting beside defence counsel."

The information that the dispatcher transmits to you in a radio call is considered "hearsay," and any information received from the dispatcher over the radio does not constitute reasonable grounds. The only exception surrounds outstanding warrants mentioned above. Why? The dispatcher has no way of knowing if the caller on the 911 phone line is telling the truth, or if the caller's information is correct.

Note: A recent Supreme Court of Canada decision has stated that police officers may enter a dwelling based solely on information obtained from a 911 emergency call.

Experienced officers will tell you that frequently the situation at the scene is different from the radio call information. For example:

1. "Attention all units. Respond to 21 Elvin St. Report of shots fired."
   The dispatcher is asking any available unit to respond, due to the urgency of the call. However, radio calls such as these are often discovered to be just cars backfiring.

2. "Unit 4, see the complainant at 58 Sumach St. Holding one for sexual assault."

   The radio dispatcher is sending unit 4 to 58 Sumach St. because someone has arrested a person for a sexual assault. However, most citizens don't know the laws well and the person being held by the citizen could in reality have exposed himself to the complainant's children. This is a less serious offence than sexual assault; there is no power of arrest for a citizen for the offence of indecent exposure.

3. "Old Clothes 2, attend The Selby at Queen and Broadview for a biker fight. Report of whips and chains being used."

   When Old Clothes 2 arrives at the scene there is no fight and no complainant. Passersby and residents of the area have seen nothing. The call is described as possibly "phony."

SAMPLE REPORTS: DETAILS OF THE OFFENCE SECTION

The Record of Arrest

The record of arrest tells the story of the arrest. It describes the chronological sequence of events. Officers often write a similar introduction, or a standard opening, which allows the writer to insert the following information in sequence:

1. time of involvement;

2. day of week;

3. month, day, year;

4. names of officers;

5. duty at time;

6. officer's location (if important);

7. source of information;

8. location of incident; and

9. nature of incident.

Once the reader knows how you became involved, the chain of events unfolds in chronological order. If an injury occurs to you, your partner, the prisoner, or anyone else, describe how it happened. Record the injuries, any treatment received, the name of the practitioner treating the injuries, and at what facility treatment was administered. When writing a record of arrest, always consider the facts in issue, or the elements of the offence. What evidence must be used to prove guilt beyond a reasonable doubt in a court of law?

Sample Record of Arrest

On Wed., 23 Jan. 1999, at approx 23:15, officers Rappah and Hyrnk were on routine patrol in scout car 5514 traveling W/B on Elgin St. west of Park Rd. At this time the officers observed a vehicle, a 1996 Toyota Celica, licence AKA 333, travelling E/B on Elgin St. The vehicle was swerving from the E/B lane into the W/B lane of traffic.

P.C. Rappah, who was operating the scout car, turned the police unit around into the E/B lane and proceeded to attempt to pull over the above-mentioned vehicle.

P.C. Rappah positioned the patrol car next to the accused's vehicle as Officer Hyrnk motioned for the driver of the Celica to pull over. The driver of the Celica ignored the officers and nearly struck the scout car at approx 23:17 as she turned her head toward the officers.

P.C. Rappah slowed the scout car and followed the Celica at a safe distance of approx 15 feet (or 4.5 m). The officers observed the Celica swerve five times from one side of the E/B lanes to the other. At times the Celica reached speeds of 80 km/h in the 50 km/h zone, and then slowed to 40 km/h.

At approx 23:20 the Celica stopped at the stop sign T intersection at Elgin St. and Garden St. At this time the officers approached the vehicle on foot and motioned the driver of the vehicle to roll down her window. The driver could not locate the knob to roll the window down.

After several attempts, she opened the driver's door and fell onto the roadway. The accused smelled strongly of what appeared to be an alcoholic beverage. Her eyes were glassy and bloodshot, and her speech was slurred.

Once P.C. Hyrnk assisted the driver to her feet, she was asked to identify herself. She did so at 23:24, with a valid Ontario driver's licence, class G, as Josie Dee, DOB 23 Jan. 1980, of 185 Royal Drive, Brantford, ON. The accused also produced ownership and insurance in the same name of Josie Dee. She had difficulty locating her identification as she dropped her wallet on the ground and upon recovering the wallet searched for approx 2 minutes to locate the identification and papers requested by P.C. Hyrnk.

At approx 23:27, the accused was arrested for impaired driving by P.C. Hyrnk, and a breath sample suitable for analysis was demanded by the officer. She was read her rights to counsel at approx 23:28 by P.C. Hyrnk. At approx 23:34, she was searched by the arresting officer and placed in the rear of scout car 5514 to be driven to headquarters for a breath test.

At approx 23:36, a tow truck was ordered to impound the Celica for safe keeping. P.C. White, assigned to 5516, stood by the Celica until the tow truck arrived. The officer searched the vehicle at 23:44 and awaited the tow truck. The tow truck towed the vehicle to Byers Pound at approx 01:02, Thurs., 24 Jan. 1999.

The arresting officers left the arrest location at approx 23:38 and arrived at headquarters with the accused at approx 23:45. At approx 02:20, Thurs., 24 Jan. 1999, the accused was turned over to P.C.

Theriault, the Breathalyzer technician. The accused was returned from the breath test at approx 03:03, with readings of 250 mgs and 230 mgs. The accused was charged with impaired driving and over 80 mgs of alcohol per 100 ml of blood.

The accused was released by Sgt. Wickendon at approx 04:40, on an 8.2, with a court date of 12 June 1999.

Sample General Occurrence Report—Theft—Stolen Property

On Friday, 26 Feb. 1999, at approx 14:30, P.C. Oliviera attended Mohawk College, Brantford Campus regarding the theft of money. Upon arrival at the main front doors of the college, the complainant, Mr. Abdul Ali, reported that his money had been removed from his wallet while he was in the cafeteria. Mr. Ali stated that at approx 13:40, he purchased a cup of coffee and proceeded to the condiment stand adjacent to the cash register, where he added cream and sugar to his coffee.

While doing so, he placed his wallet, which he had been holding in his hand, on said stand. Mr. Ali then sat in the south side of the cafeteria, next to the courtyard. At approx 13:50, the complainant realized that he was no longer in possession of his wallet. When he returned to the condiment stand, he observed his wallet where he had left it; however, upon checking the contents, he realized that $40 was missing. The denominations of the bills were: one $20 bill, one $10 bill, and two $5 bills. The money cannot be identified.

The investigating officer canvassed occupants in the cafeteria, as well as cafeteria staff, with negative results. There are no suspects at this time. The investigation is continuing.

The Break and Enter Report

Usually the police arrive at the scene, interview the complainant, and obtain a brief description and account of what happened. The three most important questions to be answered upon arrival at the scene are:

1. Is the suspect(s) still present?

2. Are any weapons present? and

3. Is anyone injured?

The police then conduct a physical investigation of the scene and request any assistance that is necessary and/or available. For example, unit detectives, a SOCO officer, or a member of the Forensic Identification Unit may be requested to attend the scene.

While the uniform officer who received the radio call awaits the arrival of specialized units, the complainant can be interviewed more thoroughly to determine additional details. In the report, the same introductory format that was used in the sample record of arrest can be used.

The next paragraph contains a brief account of who the complainant is and what he or she says concerning the matter. The paragraph following that discusses any physical evidence. A break and enter report often includes separate supplementary reports, which contain information such as:

◆ lists of stolen property, with complete descriptions and the value of the property;

◆ statements made by witnesses and the complainant;

◆ evidence; and

◆ any followup investigation reports.

In a break and enter investigation, the scene is reconstructed. Attempts are made to learn the method of entry, the point of entry, and the *modus operandi* (MO). The point of entry is the location where entrance was gained. The point of entry is important because it often yields physical evidence. The time is narrowed down as much as possible, and potential suspects are questioned.

To reconstruct the crime, inferences are made. As discussed previously, these inferences must be identified in the report as inferences, not as facts. Often it is not possible to state the exact tool or weapon used in a crime. The following are examples of inferences:

◆ "Based on the pry marks on the wooden frame of the rear basement window, and the discovery of the window, covered with fingerprints, removed from its original position in the frame onto the ground, the investigating officer believes that the window was the point of entry."

◆ "From the pry marks in the wooden frame of the window, it appears as if a prying instrument, possibly a screwdriver, was used to gain entrance."

Sample Break and Enter Report

On Fri., 30 July 1999, at approx 03:18, P.C.s Aliza and Brown, while on routine patrol in Zone 1, received a radio call to attend 187 Fairmount Dr. regarding a B & E. While en route to the above-mentioned address, at approx 03:22, the officers noticed a late-model blue Chevrolet, licence AAFG 128, travelling at a high speed down the alley to the rear of the east side of Fairmount Dr. There appeared to be two male/white occupants in the vehicle.

Upon arrival at 187 Fairmount Dr., at approx 03:24, the officers observed the front door open at 185 Fairmount Dr. A female was standing in the doorway and waving at the officers. When the officers approached her, she identified herself verbally as Terry Adams, DOB 03 Apr. 1982. She stated that her parents owned the home at 187 Fairmount Dr. and were away for a 2-week vacation.

Ms Adams reported that she had locked the house on Thurs., 29 July, at approx 18:45, and left home to visit friends. When she returned home at approx 03:10, on Fri., 30 July, she observed that the house was in darkness, even though she had left several lights on before she left. She did not enter the home. At approx 03:12, Ms Adams telephoned 911 from the neighbour's house at 185 Fairmount Dr.

P.C. Brown took Ms Adams to the neighbour's at 185 Fairmount Dr. at approx 03:30. Backup units were called at approx 03:31 to assist P.C. Aliza with a search of the premises.

At approx 03:33 P.C.s #347 and #810 arrived. The premises were searched with negative results—no suspects were located on the scene. The rear basement laundry room window was broken. Broken glass rested on the surrounding grass, as well as on the interior and exterior window ledges. This appears to have been the point of entry.

The living room seemed to have been ransacked, whereas the remainder of the house was undisturbed.

At approx 03:50, Ms Adams returned to 187 Fairmount Dr. in the company of P.C. Brown. She observed the living room from the front hallway and stated that the living room had been in perfect condition when she left the night before. From her view in the hallway, Ms Adams believed that the silver chest, containing a quantity of sterling silver, was missing, and perhaps also her father's coin collection. Ms Adams was unable to provide a description, or an estimated value, of the missing property. A supplementary report will be submitted upon the return of the owners, Ms Adams's parents, Doris and Albert Adams.

At approx 04:00, P.C. Brown notified the SOCO officer, P.C. Leonard, to attend the scene. She arrived at approx 04:12 and conducted a search of the dwelling. She located one fingerprint at the point of entry, on a piece of glass. For further details, see P.C. Leonard's supplementary report.

At approx 04:30, the neigbours were checked with negative results. No one answered their door bells. (Day shift, Zone 1 officer will attempt to locate witnesses and a supplementary report will be submitted with the results).

The late-model blue Chevrolet, licence AAFG 128 (observed driving in the alley as the investigating officers approached the crime scene) is registered to a Paul Starr of 122 Fairmount Dr. Mr. Starr's address was checked at approx 04:40 with negative results. No vehicle was parked in the alley and no one answered the door. The complainant was advised. The investigation is continuing.

EXERCISE

■ **EXERCISE 5.6   BREAK AND ENTER REPORT**

1. Examine the sample break and enter report. Identify the facts, the inferences (if any), and the opinions (if any).

2. Why are the addresses of 185 Fairmount Dr. and 187 Fairmount Dr. repeatedly mentioned in the report?

3. Why does the report state: "The living room seemed to have been ransacked"?

(Exercise 5.6 is continued on the next page.)

(Exercise 5.6 continued ...)

4. Why was Ms Adams not taken into the living room to identify the missing items?

5. You may have noticed that a good report is not a piece of literary art. Make a list of what you have noticed about report writing, having read the samples in this textbook.

CONTACT CARDS

The collection of information is an important part of police work. Information exists on computer systems, microfiche, in boxes, and in filing cabinets. A contact card is a pocket-sized report containing information that is written by an officer who has experienced a contact with an individual. Contact cards are not evidence of a criminal record, or even that the individual is involved in criminal activities.

Let's examine what contact cards may say about a person. An individual may have amassed 10 contact cards over a three-year period. This indicates that the person is possibly a criminal who has never been caught, or is perhaps a person associating with the criminal element.

If an individual has accumulated only one contact card over three years, it might show that the person was in the wrong place at the wrong time, or that the person has nothing to do with any police matter. Perhaps the person keeps late hours and was simply in a public place at 4 o'clock in the morning. Why would an officer submit a contact card concerning the latter incident? The information may be useful if, for example, a person were reported missing, or if a break and enter occurred near that time and date. The business of police work deals with the collection of information, and contact cards are a method of recording data that could be helpful.

NOTES ON COMPLETING THE FOLLOWING EXERCISES

When checking your report, make sure that every detail mentioned is clear and concise. Check the report, pretending that you have no information about the offence. When using pronouns—such as "he," "she," "them," "they," and "it"—ensure that there is no confusion over who or what is meant.

The complainant and the victim may be different people. The complainant is the person making the report. The victim is the person who suffers a loss. For example: In a break and enter, a neighbour, looking after the victim's home, reports the B & E, because the homeowner is away on holidays. The neighbour is the complainant; the homeowner is the victim. The first investigating officer makes an initial report based on the information that the complainant furnishes. This report, as with all reports, receives a general occurrence number from the records department. When the victim returns from holidays, the police must be notified and a supplementary report will be made, since only the victim would be able to provide a full list of property missing, with a complete description. This supplementary report will have the same occurrence number written on it by the second officer receiving the report. The second officer contacts the records department to obtain the general occurrence number.

Note: Any officer can submit the supplementary report. It does not have to be written by the original officer attending the first call by the neighbour.

A variety of reports are used in the exercises that follow.

DETAILS OF THE OFFENCE SECTION EXERCISES

1. Read the following sample details of the offence narratives.

2. Underline and identify each error. Make a note of the error above the underlined section.

3. In your memo book, rewrite the reports with your corrections.

■ EXERCISE 5.7   MISSING PERSON REPORT

EXERCISE

Try to locate five errors.

Note: Relevant information is recorded in the boxed area of a missing person report. There are boxed areas for a complete description of the missing person, and a section for time and date last seen.

At the a/m time on the a/m date, the writer attended 12 Bluemont Ave. regarding a missing person. Upon arrival, the complainant, Mrs. Darlene Monture, reported that her 15-year-old daughter left the house following a disagreement. Mrs. Monture was drunk and the house was in disarray. She was upset about her boyfriend.

Mrs. Monture reported that her daughter has gone missing on several previous occasions. Police records substantiate this information. When last located she was found at the boyfriend's address. This address was checked with negative results. The investigation is continuing.

■ EXERCISE 5.8   FOUND PROPERTY REPORT

EXERCISE

Try to locate four errors.

Note: Found property is kept by the property section of the service until claimed. Property is secured in a locked, caged area. Each piece of property has a property tag attached to it, which identifies the property, the circumstances, and the officer who submitted the property. If not claimed, the property will often be sold in a police auction.

The complainant reports that between the above-mentioned times and date she was walking E/B on Pacific Ave. outside #537. At this time, she observed a plain gold wedding band with no inscription. I seized the property at approx 13:50 (see property tag # 17391). The writer canvassed the area for witnesses or owner with negative results.

EXERCISE

Try to locate six errors.

Note: A complete description of the bicycle is placed in the boxed areas. The serial number is the most important piece of information. Without the serial number, it is almost impossible to locate or identify the bicycle. Often the thief changes the appearance of the bicycle shortly after the theft so that the owner is unable to make an identification.

> The complainant reports that he parked his bicycle outside of "Jim's Joint," a local hang-out for drifters. When he returned, the bicycle was gone. Although the complainant had a bicycle lock, he foolishly failed to use it. Suspects include any young person who frequents "Jim's Joint."

EXERCISE

■ EXERCISE 5.10 BREAK AND ENTER (AKA B & E) REPORT

Try to locate six errors.

Note: This is the most common occurrence report that an officer will write. According to statistics, it also has the highest unsolved rate of any crime. Although television and movies lead you to believe that arrests from B & Es in progress frequently occur, in reality they are rare.

> The complainant reports that his home was broken into while he was at work because when he left for work at 06:30 on the a/m date, all was in order and when he returned home he observed the front door was wide open. He entered the house and saw that it had been ransacked so he phoned the police and then officers arrived at the scene at approx 18:20. The POE appeared to be through the rear basement window, into the laundry room then the SOCO officer was notified at approx 18:50 and she arrived at approx 19:10. (For information concerning fingerprints and tool marks, see her report.)
>
> A quantity of cash amounting to $500 was taken, as well as jewelry and liquor. For details of property stolen, see supplementary report. The neighbours were canvassed at approx 19:40 by P.C. Shadib. Ms Alecia Skowiskowski of 189 Fairmount Rd. reported seeing two rounders run out of the front door at approx 12:30. Ms Skowiskowski described the youths as: Suspect #1: M/W, 5'10", 170#, muscular

(Exercise 5.10 is continued on the next page.)

(Exercise 5.10 continued ...)

build, short brown wavy hair, clean shaven, eyeglasses, wearing blue jeans, black T shirt with some sort of writing on it, and a baseball cap. Suspect #2: M/Brown, 6'1", 160#, thin build, wearing blue jeans and a dark jacket.

Ms Skowiskowski can identify suspect #1 but not suspect #2 because she did not see him clearly. Arrangements have been made for the witness to attend the Forensic Identification Unit to look at photographs on Thurs., 12 May 2000, at 09:00. A supplementary report will be submitted with the results.

Note: Complainants should be advised that they should not enter their home if a similar incident should occur again. They should immediately leave the area and notify the police from a safe location—the suspect(s) could be inside.

This occurrence requires some supplementary reports on your part:

1. A list of property stolen, with full descriptions.

2. A report from the SOCO officer. (The "scenes of crime officer" provides certain services that were previously offered only by the identification units, or forensic identification units. SOCO are uniform officers who have been trained to collect physical evidence such as fingerprints and physical matches. These uniform officers are attached to every shift and have taken some of the burden off identification units. Serious crimes such as homicides are investigated by identification officers, not SOCO officers.)

3. A report with the results of the photo lineup.

4. A report with any further information obtained by the original investigating officer or any other officer.

■ EXERCISE 5.11   ALARM CALL REPORT

Try to locate four errors.

On the a/m time and date we attended 146 Allan Blvd. regarding an alarm call. Upon arrival at 03:00 the premises were checked and no signs of entry were visible.

At approx 04:06 the key holder, Alan Anderson, attended. Backup units were called.

(Exercise 5.11 is continued on the next page.)

EXERCISE

(Exercise 5.11 continued ...)

> The premises were checked by all officers with negative re-sults. This is the tenth false alarm received at this location in the past two months.

Note: In this case, there were no signs of entry, so the keyholder was contacted, attended the scene, and unlocked the premises. The officers then searched the interior. Backup is usually called for assistance at an alarm call, depending on the circumstances. The rules and regulations of many police services state that an officer attending an alarm must wait for backup before searching.

The keyholder is an employee of the premises who has a key to the property. Records are kept at the local police station listing every business in the division, particulars of each business, and the name and contact phone number of the keyholder.

Officers at the scene of an alarm call ask the radio dispatcher to call the police station, so that station staff may look up the listing and then telephone the keyholder. The keyholder proceeds to the scene and unlocks the door. Some keyholders may not wish to be present inside the building while it is being searched.

A special note about officer safety: Just because you cannot locate any signs of entry does not mean that the suspect, or suspects, are not inside. Don't become complacent. Likewise, even though over 90 percent of alarm calls are false, you should treat every alarm as if it were real. For example, it is often not possible to check a roof for a POE.

■ **EXERCISE 5.12 RECORD OF ARREST: CHARGE—CAUSING A DISTURBANCE ON OR NEAR A PUBLIC PLACE**

In your *Criminal Code*, locate the section on causing a disturbance. Notice the "elements of the offence" or the "facts in issue" that must be proved to obtain a conviction. You will be asked questions at the end of this example.

Note: In the record of arrest boxed section, there is a box for a CPIC check. Checking this box ensures that every person under arrest has been checked through CPIC. In the past, embarrassing situations have arisen when charged persons for whom warrants are outstanding have been released. Besides feeling embarrassed, you could also be charged with "neglect of duty" under the *Police Services Act*.

Try to locate eight errors.

> On the a/m time and date, my partner and I were at Tim Horton's Donut shop investigating an unrelated occurrence. At

(Exercise 5.12 is continued on the next page.)

(Exercise 5.12 continued ...)

approx 01:17 the accused enters the shop as drunk as could be. He was loud and obnoxious, screaming obscene language at the top of his lungs. He screamed, "You f-ckin' pigs* have nothin' better to do than get free coffee!" He then commenced to swear, saying "You G-d da-ned @#%* are wasting the taxpayer's money. Why don't you go out and catch some bad guys?" This behaviour continues for approx 5 minutes.

During this time, I observe that patrons in the donut shop appeared to be shocked. One elderly female quickly sat down and commenced to fan herself with a newspaper. Several patrons cover their mouths with their hands and gasped. Then she left quickly.

I decided to take the loudmouth's advice and arrested him at 01:25, cuffed him, and transported him to the station. At 02:10 he was charged with causing a disturbance. He was released at 02:45 by Sgt. Hoi with a court date of 24 Nov. 1999.

* Note: In a real report, the exact language used is recorded.

Questions

1. According to the *Criminal Code*, what must be proved to support a conviction for causing a disturbance? In other words, what are the facts in issue, or elements of the offence?

2. Were the facts in issue proven in this report? Support your answer.

(Exercise 5.12 is continued on the next page.)

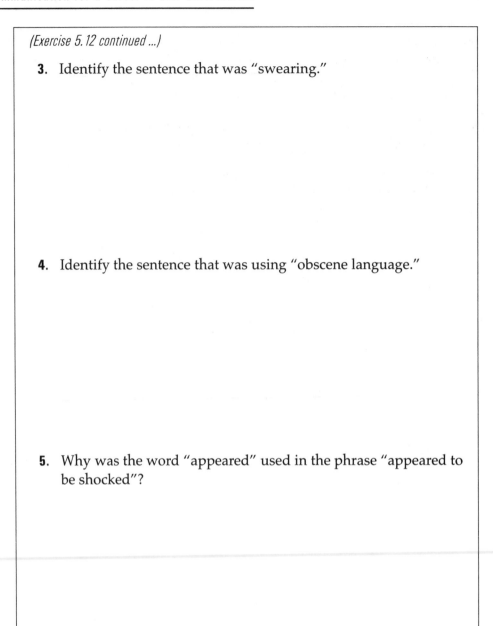

(Exercise 5.12 continued ...)

3. Identify the sentence that was "swearing."

4. Identify the sentence that was using "obscene language."

5. Why was the word "appeared" used in the phrase "appeared to be shocked"?

Sometimes writing reports can be extremely difficult. For example, if you attend the scene of a fight with a large number of people involved, events may occur very quickly and be very confusing. Your report, however, must make sense. Due to the nature of the scene, you probably would not have had the opportunity to make notes in your memo book. The time period when you cannot make notes may even cover hours.

The communications area of your police service will be able to assist you, because a record will exist for all of the times you notified the radio dispatcher of various actions surrounding the event. From the communications section you can obtain information such as:

◆   the time R/C was dispatched;

◆   the time you arrived at the scene;

◆ the times of all of your requests for such things as backup, the ambulance crew, the fire department, specialized units (for example, homicide, sexual assault, hit and run, photo unit, fraud), the supervisor, and the detectives; and

◆ the arrival and departure times of any requested units (as these units arrive and depart, they notify the dispatcher).

Sometimes you may not know what happened. For example, if you are rendered unconscious, all you can write about (and testify about in court) is what occurred before you lost consciousness and what occurred after you regained consciousness. A report contains only factual information, not speculations.

REPORT WRITING CHECKLIST

		Yes	No
1.	Is the spelling correct?	____	____
2.	Is the grammar correct?	____	____
3.	Are the pronouns clear?	____	____
4.	Are the sentences short and simple?	____	____
5.	Do the sentences begin with the subject?	____	____
6.	Is there only one idea per paragraph?	____	____
7.	Are the lengths of the paragraphs suitable?	____	____
8.	Is the report written in the third person?	____	____
9.	Are active verbs used?	____	____
10.	Is the past tense of the verb used?	____	____
11.	Is the report written in chronological order from the point of view of the reporter?	____	____
12.	Have the facts in issue been established?	____	____
13.	Is the report objective, and free of judgments and bias?	____	____
14.	Has the reporter differentiated between facts and inferences?	____	____
15.	Are descriptions presented in an organized fashion?	____	____
16.	Is the report accurate? Have the "5 W's" been covered?	____	____
17.	Is the report concise, with no irrelevant detail?	____	____
18.	Is the report professional, without slang, and does it reflect positively on the writer?	____	____
19.	Does the reader understand what has happened?	____	____
20.	Is the report neat and legible?	____	____

SAMPLE REPORTS FOR PRACTICE

Record of Arrest Report

name of accused		alias
address		arrest number
city/town	Province	CPIC check
postal code		arrest log
phone number	occupation	business phone
date, time arrested		location of arrest	Zone/ patrol area
charge		type of premises
date of birth	age	place of birth
sex	race	height	weight	build
hair		eyes
visible marks, scars, tattoos, deformities		drug user
clothing		
identification of accused		taken to hospital	transported by
complaint of injuries or illnesses		doctor
		rights read by
complainant Address		home phone
date of birth	age	business phone
injuries		
mental/physical condition of victim		
vehicle used		vehicle action
deposition of vehicle		seized for evidence

Details of offence

Details of offence (continued)

property taken from accused	booking officer:
	time, date booked
supervisor's name	arresting officers:
supervisor's signature	arresting officers' signature
vacation dates of arresting officers	

Record of Arrest Report

name of accused	alias
address	arrest number
city/town / Province	CPIC check
postal code	arrest log
phone number / occupation	business phone
date, time arrested	location of arrest / Zone/ patrol area
charge	type of premises
date of birth / age	place of birth
sex / race / height	weight / build
hair	eyes
visible marks, scars, tattoos, deformities	drug user
clothing	
identification of accused	taken to hospital / transported by
complaint of injuries or illnesses	doctor / rights read by
complainant Address	home phone
date of birth / age	business phone
injuries	
mental/physical condition of victim	
vehicle used	vehicle action
deposition of vehicle	seized for evidence
Details of offence	

Details of offence (continued)

property taken from accused	booking officer:
	time, date booked
supervisor's name	arresting officers:
supervisor's signature	arresting officers' signature
vacation dates of arresting officers	

Record of Arrest Report

name of accused			alias	
address			arrest number	
city/town		Province	CPIC check	
postal code			arrest log	
phone number		occupation	business phone	
date, time arrested			location of arrest	Zone/ patrol area
charge			type of premises	
date of birth		age	place of birth	
sex	race	height	weight	build
hair			eyes	
visible marks, scars, tattoos, deformities				drug user
clothing				-

identification of accused		taken to hospital	transported by
complaint of injuries or illnesses		doctor	
		rights read by	
complainant Address		home phone	
date of birth	age	business phone	
injuries			
mental/physical condition of victim			

vehicle used	vehicle action
deposition of vehicle	seized for evidence

Details of offence

Details of offence (continued)

property taken from accused	booking officer:
	time, date booked
supervisor's name	arresting officers:
supervisor's signature	arresting officers' signature
vacation dates of arresting officers	

Record of Arrest Report

name of accused		alias	
address		arrest number	
city/town	Province	CPIC check	
postal code		arrest log	
phone number	occupation	business phone	
date, time arrested		location of arrest	Zone/ patrol area
charge		type of premises	
date of birth	age	place of birth	
sex	race	height	weight	build
hair		eyes	
visible marks, scars, tattoos, deformities		drug user	
clothing			
identification of accused		taken to hospital	transported by
complaint of injuries or illnesses		doctor	
		rights read by	
complainant Address		home phone	
date of birth	age	business phone	
injuries			
mental/physical condition of victim			
vehicle used		vehicle action	
deposition of vehicle		seized for evidence	
Details of offence			

Details of offence (continued)

property taken from accused	booking officer:
	time, date booked
supervisor's name	arresting officers:
supervisor's signature	arresting officers' signature
vacation dates of arresting officers	

General Occurrence Report

type of offence		time	date
location of offence		zone	
complainant/victim	DOB	age	
address postal code		phone (home & business)	
reported by (include relationship to complainant/victim)		DOB	
address postal code		phone number (home & business)	
witnesses	DOB	address	
point of entry			
suspect alias		DOB	
address		phone	
description tattoos/birthmarks/deformities			
vehicle involved			
injuries	hospital doctor		
property taken	next of kin notified		
condition of victim			
Details of offence			

P.C. name	signature
	badge number
supervisor's name	time/date of report
follow-up unit	

General Occurrence Report

type of offence			time	date
location of offence			zone	
complainant/victim		DOB	age	
address			phone (home & business)	
postal code				
reported by (include relationship to complainant/victim)			DOB	
address			phone number (home & business)	
postal code				
witnesses		DOB	address	
point of entry				
suspect			DOB	
alias				
address			phone	
description				
tattoos/birthmarks/deformities				
vehicle involved				
injuries		hospital		
		doctor		
property taken				
		next of kin notified		
condition of victim				

Details of offence

P.C. name	signature
	badge number
supervisor's name	time/date of report
follow-up unit	

General Occurrence Report

type of offence		time	date
location of offence		zone	
complainant/victim	DOB	age	
address postal code		phone (home & business)	
reported by (include relationship to complainant/victim)		DOB	
address postal code		phone number (home & business)	
witnesses	DOB	address	
point of entry			
suspect alias		DOB	
address		phone	
description tattoos/birthmarks/deformities			
vehicle involved			
injuries		hospital doctor	
property taken		next of kin notified	
condition of victim			
Details of offence			

P.C. name	signature
	badge number
supervisor's name	time/date of report
follow-up unit	

General Occurrence Report

type of offence		time	date
location of offence		zone	
complainant/victim	DOB	age	
address postal code		phone (home & business)	
reported by (include relationship to complainant/victim)		DOB	
address postal code		phone number (home & business)	
witnesses	DOB	address	
point of entry			
suspect alias		DOB	
address		phone	
description tattoos/birthmarks/deformities			
vehicle involved			
injuries	hospital doctor		
property taken	next of kin notified		
condition of victim			
Details of offence			

P.C. name	signature
	badge number
supervisor's name	time/date of report
follow-up unit	

Missing Person Report

name of missing person		alias	is missing person a youth
address			

city/town		province	CPIC check	
postal code			arrest log, hospitals checked	
phone number			business phone	

school name, address, grade, if student		location where last seen	zone/ patrol area
date/time last seen		date/time reported	

date of birth		age	place of birth	
sex	race	height	marital status	weight	build

hair	eyes

visible marks, scars, tattoos, deformities	drug user
clothing	

possible cause of absence

possible destination	has person been drinking or taking drugs	
mental/physical condition	has person been missing before	how often
	time/date, & where located, if missing before	
	relationship to missing person	
complainant/reported by		

complainant address	home phone	business phone

has missing person ever been fingerprinted	if yes, when, where	personal habits
injuries		

licence plate & description of vehicle, if driving	places checked by complainant prior to notifying police
amount of money believed to be in possession of missing person	credit cards believed to be in possession of missing person

<u>Details</u>

date/time report submitted	report submitted by
supervisor's name	reporting officer's signature
supervisor's signature	

Missing Person Report

name of missing person		alias	is missing person a youth
address			

city/town		province	CPIC check	
postal code			arrest log, hospitals checked	

phone number	business phone	

school name, address, grade, if student	location where last seen	zone/ patrol area

date/time last seen	date/time reported

date of birth		age	place of birth	
sex	race	height	marital status	weight	build
hair				eyes	

visible marks, scars, tattoos, deformities	drug user

clothing

possible cause of absence

possible destination	has person been drinking or taking drugs	
mental/physical condition	has person been missing before	how often
	time/date, & where located, if missing before	
	relationship to missing person	
complainant/reported by		

complainant address	home phone	business phone

has missing person ever been fingerprinted	if yes, when, where	personal habits
injuries		

licence plate & description of vehicle, if driving	places checked by complainant prior to notifying police

amount of money believed to be in possession of missing person	credit cards believed to be in possession of missing person

Details

date/time report submitted	report submitted by
supervisor's name	reporting officer's signature
supervisor's signature	

Missing Person Report

name of missing person	alias	is missing person a youth
address		

city/town	province	CPIC check
postal code		arrest log, hospitals checked

phone number	business phone

school name, address, grade, if student	location where last seen	zone/ patrol area

date/time last seen	date/time reported

date of birth	age	place of birth

sex	race	height	marital status	weight	build
hair				eyes	

visible marks, scars, tattoos, deformities	drug user

clothing

possible cause of absence

possible destination	has person been drinking or taking drugs	
mental/physical condition	has person been missing before	how often
	time/date, & where located, if missing before	
	relationship to missing person	
complainant/reported by		

complainant address	home phone	business phone

has missing person ever been fingerprinted	if yes, when, where	personal habits
injuries		

licence plate & description of vehicle, if driving	places checked by complainant prior to notifying police

amount of money believed to be in possession of missing person	credit cards believed to be in possession of missing person

Details

date/time report submitted	report submitted by
supervisor's name	reporting officer's signature
supervisor's signature	

Missing Person Report

name of missing person		alias	is missing person a youth
address			

city/town	province	CPIC check	
postal code		arrest log, hospitals checked	
phone number		business phone	
school name, address, grade, if student		location where last seen	zone/ patrol area
date/time last seen		date/time reported	

date of birth		age	place of birth		
sex	race	height	marital status	weight	build
hair			eyes		

visible marks, scars, tattoos, deformities	drug user
clothing	
possible cause of absence	

possible destination	
	has person been drinking or taking drugs
mental/physical condition	has person been missing before / how often
	time/date, & where located, if missing before
	relationship to missing person
complainant/reported by	

complainant address	home phone	business phone

has missing person ever been fingerprinted	if yes, when, where	personal habits
injuries		

licence plate & description of vehicle, if driving	places checked by complainant prior to notifying police
amount of money believed to be in possession of missing person	credit cards believed to be in possession of missing person

Details

date/time report submitted	report submitted by
supervisor's name	reporting officer's signature
supervisor's signature	

Supplementary Occurrence Report

type of occurrence	occurrence number
location	time/date

occurrence details

officer's name/number	officer's signature
time/date of report	division

Supplementary Occurrence Report

type of occurrence	occurrence number
location	time/date

occurrence details

officer's name/number	officer's signature
time/date of report	division

Supplementary Occurrence Report

type of occurrence	occurrence number
location	time/date

occurrence details

officer's name/number	officer's signature
time/date of report	division

Supplementary Occurrence Report

type of occurrence	occurrence number
location	time/date

occurrence details

officer's name/number	officer's signature
time/date of report	division

Contact Card

name		alias	
address		CPIC check	
city/town	province	postal code	
phone number	occupation/school	business phone	
date, time of contact		location	zone/ patrol area
Sex	race	height	weight	build
hair		eyes	
visible marks, scars, tattoos, deformities			
clothing			

Details of contact

officer's name and number	officer's signature
division	time/date

Contact Card

name			alias		
address			CPIC check		
city/town		province	postal code		
phone number		occupation/school	business phone		
date, time of contact			location		zone/ patrol area
Sex	race	height	weight	build	
hair			eyes		
visible marks, scars, tattoos, deformities					
clothing					

Details of contact

officer's name and number	officer's signature
division	time/date

Contact Card

name		alias	
address		CPIC check	
city/town	province	postal code	
phone number	occupation/school	business phone	
date, time of contact		location	zone/ patrol area
Sex	race	height	weight	build
hair		eyes	
visible marks, scars, tattoos, deformities			
clothing			

Details of contact

officer's name and number	officer's signature
division	time/date

Contact Card

name		alias	
address		CPIC check	
city/town	province	postal code	
phone number	occupation/school	business phone	
date, time of contact		location	zone/ patrol area
Sex	race	height	weight	build
hair		eyes	
visible marks, scars, tattoos, deformities			
clothing			
Details of contact			
officer's name and number		officer's signature	
division		time/date	

CHAPTER 6
Memo Books

GENERAL DESCRIPTION

Memo books are also known as duty notebooks or field notes. The memo book holds the recorded details of circumstances that an officer encounters during a tour of duty. The notes are made while the events are fresh in the officer's mind. These notes enable the officer to write accurate reports. The times for every activity are recorded in the 24-hour clock system. There are many specific rules for memo books, which are identified in the box below. An explanation is also provided for each rule.

MEMO BOOK RULES

Note: These rules are inflexible.

Rule	Reason
Memo books are notepads of lined paper. Each page usually has a printed number on the bottom of the page. *Never rip a page out of your memo book.* If the pages are not numbered, number them yourself.	The pages are numbered to ensure that the notes are not altered or tampered with once they have been written. If you have a page missing from your memo book, it becomes a big issue in court: What happened to it? What are you trying to hide? Your credibility sinks.
Notes are handwritten in pen, never pencil.	In most police services, official police reports are written in black ink. Black pen photocopies better than blue or any other colour. Pencil is never used because pencilled notes could easily be changed.
At the start of the shift, you list important details concerning anything outstanding, any serious event that is in progress at the time of shift change, wanted persons, bulletins, relevant CPIC information, and any special attention memos.	This information may prove useful during your tour of duty.

Rule	Reason
There are no open spaces or missed lines—*every line is filled in without gaps*. Some services follow a standard rule of leaving one or two lines between shift entries. These blank lines have to be consistent throughout the memo book; otherwise, in court the judge will question the lack of consistency.	Open spaces suggest that you have left room to add information at a later time. This is not an acceptable procedure. Leaving a line empty makes the same suggestion. Again, in court your credibility will suffer and your testimony may not be allowed. If it is allowed, it may be regarded with suspicion.
The date is recorded and underlined at top of every shift with information concerning: officer's name, badge number, time paraded for duty, escort (that is, partner, if applicable), unit assigned to, nature of duty, car number or beat assigned, portable radio number, weather conditions, road conditions, number of radio calls, number of arrests, number of tags, number of summonses, name and badge number of relieving officer. Some forces use a stamp with these headings and the officers fill in the blanks. The supervisor places the stamp immediately below his or her own signature, which is placed on the line below your signature. When your next shift starts, you can fill in some of the blanks on parade; the remainder of the blanks are completed at the end of the shift.	Dates in police work are always crucial. The information in the stamped area provides details of the shift that may be required at a later date. If you are working a 19:00-07:00 hour shift, then the date of the new day must be recorded in the memo book at 12:00 midnight.
Times for *everything* are clearly placed in the lefthand column.	Accurate times in police work are absolute necessities. Many major cases have been botched by the inaccurate recording of times. Also, for a victim of a crime, 1 minute may seem like 10 minutes. Your record of times may be helpful if a complaint is made about slow response time. Records from the dispatcher of communications will also back up your time.
Time is written in the 24-hour clock system.	Again, accuracy is the focus. The 24-hour clock system causes less confusion. You cannot mistake 02:00 for 14:00 hours.
If an error is made, *one* line is made in pen through the error and the officer writes his or her initials next to the error. The crossed-out information can still be read.	Again, nothing is hidden, erased, or altered. The reader can clearly see what was previously written, but then changed.

Rule	Reason
Complete and relevant information is recorded for every event, in chronological order. Personal comments and irrelevant information are not recorded.	If you leave some information out of your memo book, you may not remember it 18 months later when your case comes to trial. If you add information during your testimony that is not recorded in your notes, the following question may be raised: Have you fabricated this part of your testimony to create a stronger case?
Notes show all required signatures of any person throughout your shift. For example, a charged person may give you permission to allow his or her friend to drive the charged person's car home.	The charged person's signature confirms that he or she gave you permission to turn the keys over to the friend. This protects you if the friend damages the car or the like. (Of course, you'd have to check that the friend was a licensed driver, was sober, had no outstanding warrants, and was not prohibited or suspended from driving.)
The memo book that you use daily is the same memo book that you take to court. *You do not rewrite it to make a good copy!*	Some officers want to have a second memo book where the notes are neat and well organized. This is severely frowned upon by the courts and your case may be lost if this comes to light. Your testimony and your memo book may not be admitted as evidence; you may now no longer have sufficient evidence to prove the case.
Do not report off duty until your memo book is up to date.	During your time off, information may be needed from your memo book. If this information is important but the book is not updated, then no one will get the answers that are needed.
At the end of shift, record "report off duty" (some services allow the short form ROD), and on the next line write your signature. Some services write the officer's badge number and "Off Duty"—for example, "5553 Off Duty"—followed by the signature on the next line. Your signature will be on the last line of your notes for that shift.	Your signature verifies that officially your tour of duty has ended.

Rule	Reason
Some services allow you to take your memo book home, whereas other services require that you hand in your memo book at the end of the shift. Your memo book needs a supervisor's signature at the end of *every shift*.	The supervisor checks your notes and looks for any irregularities. Part of the supervisor's job is to check your work for accuracy and his or her signature will most likely prove that your notes were correct and precise. If you die before the trial, your memo books may be allowed in court, due to this checking for accuracy by the supervisor. This is a rule of evidence.
Memo books are usually stored in a secured area at the station near the parade room. For those services requiring you to leave them at the station, there are some exceptions. For example, you may have court the next morning, or you may be travelling to a location other than your station for a new assignment on your next tour of duty. Old memo books are kept in a secured storage area within the station. If you need a memo book for court, you obtain a key to the locked area and locate the needed memo book. When your court case is complete, the memo book(s) is returned to the locked area.	Memo books belong to your police service. They must also not be altered or tampered with. Securing the books assists with this goal.

FACTS ABOUT MEMO BOOKS

◆ Memo books are the property of the department for which you work. They are not your personal property.

◆ All of the information that you place on a report and/or statements will also be recorded in your memo book. Usually you refer to your memo book in order to write your report. Consistency between your notes and the report is crucial if the case goes to trial.

◆ When you are testifying, the judge may examine your memo book. The judge can give the defence lawyer permission to look at your notes before you are cross-examined by the defence counsel. You *must* allow the judge and the defence lawyer (if the judge provides permission) to read the memo book. The defence lawyer should be focusing on the information pertinent to the case before the courts. The defence, knowing that he or she will be cross-examining you as a Crown witness in a future trial, should not read in detail any notes concerning that particular event. Many officers, when appearing in court, use paperclips or two elastic bands to mark the pages that cover the events before the court. By doing this, they can clearly see if the defence lawyer removes the paperclips or elastics and starts to read other cases. If this happens to you in court, you should point out to the judge: "Excuse me, Your Honour (Worship, Lordship), but the notes beyond the paperclips pertain to a future case I am involved with and the defence lawyer is scheduled to represent the accused." The judge will ensure that the lawyer stops reading those pages.

◆   When you testify in court, you *may* use your memo book, but it is not an automatic right. Before you can get out your memo book and start reading, you *must* first obtain permission from the judge or justice of the peace. The conversation usually proceeds something like this:

> Officer: Your Honour (Worship, Lordship), may I refer to my notes to refresh my memory?
>
> Judge: When were these notes made, officer?
>
> Officer: During the investigation at various points, whenever I had an opportunity to record information.
>
> Judge: May I see those notes, officer?
>
> Officer: Yes, sir/madam.

The judge examines the notes to determine if the notes are "contemporaneous," which means that the notes were all made during the same period of time, when the officer's memory was fresh. To determine this, the judge may ask such questions as:

◆   "When did you make the notes?"

◆   "Did you make the notes from your own memory or did you consult any other officer before making the notes?" This is a touchy area. Many officers think it is wrong to follow the common practice of officers writing their memo books together. The defence counsel may ask you to explain why your description of the event is exactly the same as your partner's. Officers usually write their memo books together so that their stories will corroborate each other. This practice has received some degree of disapproval by the courts. If you do write your memo book with your partner, be truthful. Lying simply brings the defence lawyer and the judge into an attack mode. They both know that almost all police officers write their notes together. If you lie under oath or affirmation, you've had it!

◆   "Have you made any additions or deletions from the notes since you first recorded them?"

◆   "Where were you when the notes were made?"

While asking these questions, the judge looks carefully at the notes to see evidence of timeliness. Evidence of the notes being contemporaneous includes:

- ◆ the use of the same pen throughout,

- ◆ writing and spacing matching the other notes in the memo book, and

- ◆ style of notation matching other notes: same short forms used; same method of recording dates, names, descriptions, addressees, expressions; similar grammar and vocabulary.

If the judge believes that the notes are contemporaneous, then he or she *may* allow them to be used in court. It's up to the judge.

Do you have to use your memo book when testifying in court? No. However, most officers do not have a photographic memory. On a rare occasion, you will see an officer testifying in court without the aid of a memo book. Sometimes the officer is doing this so that the defence lawyer and the judge cannot look at his or her memo book. Perhaps the notes are incomplete, have spaces between the lines, or contain unprofessional details that the officer does not want discovered. Although this may not be the case, this is what the court may be thinking.

TYPE OF INFORMATION RECORDED IN MEMO BOOKS

Persons

Suspects, victims, witnesses, other persons described from head to toe: sex; race; hair—colour, style, curly, straight, length, receding hairline, neat or unkempt, and so on; height; weight; build; complexion; facial hair; facial features; eye colour and shape; glasses; nose; mouth; any distinguishing facial features; voice—accent, speech impediments, unusual words or phrases; breath smell, if any; clothing—hat, balaclava, or other method used to hide face; shirt—colour, pattern, style, dirty or clean, condition (for example, ripped); pants/shorts—same details as shirt; coat—same details as shirt; shoes—colour, style; socks; tattoos, deformities, scars, missing teeth, any other distinguishing features.

Who

Identify persons—witness, suspect, complainant, victim; correct name in full; date of birth; age; address in full; home phone number; occupation; work address and phone number; aliases; student—school; place of birth.

When

Date and time offence occurred, reported, discovered; evidence located; witnesses, victims, next of kin contacted; arrest made; when suspect released and by whom; if suspect not released, where lodged; court date of suspect.

Where

Exact location of offence (map if necessary); type of premises or area—dwelling, factory, field, roadway, and so on; location of victim, witnesses, suspects in relation to crime.

What

Type of offence; type of property involved; vehicle used, if any, or if suspect was on foot; property obtained; what occurred—suspect located and approached, entrance gained, exit from scene; what was used for identification—for example, valid Ontario driver's licence.

Why

Events leading to occurrence; cause; drug or alcohol factors; accidental; intentional.

Vehicles

Make; model; year; licence plate number, province, valtag number; colour; style (two-door, four-door, hatchback, and so on); distinguishing features or damage; value; insured; property inside vehicle.

Property Other Than Vehicles

Descriptions will vary according to type of property. May include: manufacturer; model name; model number; serial number—important information if property is likely to be recovered and identified by complainant; cost/value; age; colour; size; style; distinguishing marks; insured.

Other

Date(s) and time(s) for everything; type of incident; exact location of occurrence; persons involved; witnesses; other relevant information such as: evidence, location of evidence, time discovered, continuity of evidence; assisting officers and/or specialized units; measurements; other agencies involved—for example, fire department, ambulance unit; supervisor visiting occurrence.

REMINDERS

◆ Limit notes to relevant facts and information.

◆ When writing notes, alternate between writing and listening—it's hard to listen and write at the same time without making errors.

- Do not interrupt the speaker—if interrupted, the speaker may never return to the point where the interruption occurred.

- Ask clarifying questions when the speaker is finished his or her sentence. If you are unsure of what the speaker has said, repeat what the speaker has said using same language used by the speaker. The only way you will know that you have not misinterpreted what the speaker meant is by repeating the message back, thus obtaining verification.

- Check your notes for accuracy and required details.

SAMPLE OF A TOUR OF DUTY RECORDED IN A MEMO BOOK

Any explanations defining short forms have been placed in square [ ] brackets. In this example, the police service uses a stamp (mentioned previously) to record the information in the box below.

PC name	badge number	escort
H. Hattoff	5553	5580
time of parade	**car number/beat**	**portable radio #**
06:45	zone 5	6
unit assigned to	**number of radio calls**	**number of tags**
uniform	3	9
number of summonses	**number of arrests**	**weather conditions**
2	0	mild, 20, cloudy

road conditions	lunch	badge number of relief
dry, clear	13:00	3001

06:30	Friday 21 May 1999 Report for duty Special attention: 23 Adel Ave.—peace bond out against Jeff Smyth, held by wife Jolene Smyth. CPIC—Jehir Zahri, 14 Oct. 75,

		wanted for abduction, robbery—armed, considered dangerous;
		M/W, 5'11", 210 #, heavy build, long blond shag-style hair,
		fu-manchu, tattoo upper left forearm 2 snakes forming cross,
		possible destination sw Ont.
06:45		*Parade for duty. Sunday lecture this weekend—ethics—10:00*
06:58		*Relieve P.C. Maodus, car zone 5*
07:00		*10-8* [clear for radio calls]. *Patrol RHR* [rush hour routes]
07:43		*Observe broken down vehicle Chev. Impala lic JYE 448, on Kingston Rd. at Main, n/e corner, obstructing traffic. Assist driver, Mr. Robert Anatanasile, DOB 13 Mar/48*
08:09		*Tow truck ordered at owner's request. Direct traffic*
08:14		*Tow truck of Byers Pound arrives, Matt Hyutt operator*
08:29		*Vehicle removed*
08:34		*Patrol RHR*
09:00		*GP* [general patrol]
10:03		*R/C* [radio call], *attend 79 Hatt St. see compl't* [complainant] *re attempt theft from auto*
10:10		*On loc, compl't Sarah Whitehurst reports that she parked her vehicle at 03:30 on 21 May/99 in drive way of home at 79 Hatt St. When she approached car to go to work at 07:45 on 22 May/99 she observed the side driver's window to be shattered. Attempts were made by suspect(s) to remove car radio. Observed radio on floor of driver's floor mat, with wires still intact. Suspect(s) possibly frightened off. Ms. Whitehurst advised she did not touch anything Compl't: Ms Sarah Whitehurst, DOB 04 Apr. 80, home: 79 Hatt St, Dundas, Ont. 627-3124, bus: The Keg, 3289 King St. W, Hamilton, 575-8990. Vehicle: 1997 Toyota Camry, lic: "SARA"—personalized plate, insured. Estimated value of damage to radio—$20.00; to replace driver's side window $200.00*
10:24		*SOCO* [Scenes of Crime Officer], *P.C. Prentice, notified and requested to attend scene*
10:30		*P.C. Prentice advised ETA 11:00*
10:50		*Neighbours canvassed for info. Mr. R. Piaget, of 85 Hatt St. advised that at approx. 06:00 he let his dog out in his backyard. At that time he heard a noise which he believed to be shattering glass. His dog barked a lot. Mr. Piaget looked around at the front of his house but did not see anything unusual. Standing at the front of his*

	house where he said he was, observed that he could not have a clear view of the comp'ts car—trees obstructing the view
11:48	SOCO officer P.C. Prentice arrives. Will advise re discovery of fingerprints or other evidence. Report to be submitted
11:57	10-8. Check address re special attention—Jolene Smyth. All in order
12:10	GP
13:00	At station re lunch. Relief driver P.C. #98
14:04	Resume duty—GP
14:38	R/C attend HQ—pick up a warrant for CIB [Criminal Investigation Bureau—the detectives from the division], Wyatt Armstrong, DOB 18 Aug 76
14:46	At HQ re warrant
15:15	Leave HQ, return to stn with warrant
15:22	Hand over warrant to CIB, Sgt. Swain
15:45	Clear. Check props [properties]
16:04	Attend 11 Niagara St. see witness Julie Dunn re assault report on 12 May/99 for further info.
16:14	On loc, witness reports no new info
16:34	Clear Patrol RHR
17:16	R/C intersection of Queen and Park re car on fire
17:23	On loc traffic unit #2 on scene. Assist with traffic direction
17:26	Fire dept. on scene
18:13	All in order. Traffic unit #2 advises no longer needed
18:15	Clear. Check address re special attention—Jolene Smyth. All in order
18:39	Make way to stn re shift change
18:53	10-7 [out of service] station
19:00	Report off Duty
	Helen Hattoff P.C. 5553
	Sgt. Fitzgerald

■ EXERCISE 6.1   MEMO BOOK CORRECTIONS

EXERCISE

1. Read the memo book details that follow.
2. Underline and identify the errors.
3. Correct the errors by rewriting the notes in your memo book.

PC name	badge number	escort
J. Cartledge	577	327

time of parade	car number/beat	portable radio #
6:45pm	zone	

unit assigned to	number of radio calls	number of tags
uniform	5	

number of summonses	number of arrests	weather conditions
	1	cold, 3, cloudy

road conditions	lunch	badge number of relief
dry, clear	10:00pm	

	Friday 01/08/99
6:30pm	Report for duty
	Special attention: Commissioner Ave., youths drag racing in early
	hrs. of morning.
	Parade for duty.
	Relieve Bob, car zone 3
7:00	10-8
7:10	R/C, attend K Mart store, see John Watt, security re shoplifter. On
	loc. attend security office of K Mart. John Watt, security guard,

(Exercise 6.1 is continued on the next page.)

(Exercise 6.1 continued ...)

	advises that he has arrested one Harold Paulie, DOB 03 Mar. 70, for theft under. John Watt reports that while in the jewelry department of K Mart, he observed Mr. Paulie select a variety of jewelry and place same into a brown shopping bag. Mr. Watt followed Mr. Paulie for an extensive period of time. Then he left the store. Mr. Watt arrested the accused in the parking lot outside of the west doors of K Mart.
	Arrive at station re report.
	Arrest line notified re Mr. Paulie. 8.1 submitted and reports typed.
8:30pm	CPIC check shows Mr. Paulie wanted on a province-wide warrant for robbery.
9:00pm	Attend Mr. Paulie's address re a/m warrant.
	No response at door.
	10-8 General patrol.
9:04	R/C 31 Lawlor Ave. re noise complaint. On loc. occupant of 31 Lawlor advises that she rents the property. Advised re noise.
	10-8.
9:24pm	R/C 72 Spencer Ave. re neighbour dispute. On loc. noisy, obnoxious, mouthy neighbours verbally fighting over parking. One neighbour complains that other neighbour partially obstructs his driveway with his truck. Check driveway—truck is clear of driveway by 4 inches. Parties advised.
9:40pm	10-8. Check properties.
	Check special attention Commissioner re drag races. All in order.
9:55pm	10-8. GP.
10:01	R/C 977 Charlotte Dr. re missing prop
	On loc. compl't P. Jakowski reports missing lawn ornaments from rear garden. Check garden. Compl't advised.
10:20	10-8.
	R/C NW corner of King and Main—see ambulance crew re. one to go [one individual for arrest]. On loc. observe ambulance attendant holding her head, resting on ground in a lying position.

(Exercise 6.1 is continued on the next page.)

(Exercise 6.1 continued ...)

	Ambulance attendant, Joan Kate, DOB 3/7/60 reports that male on scene, id'd as Don Colson, DOB 9/4/59, kicked her in the stomach as she attempted to assist him with a broken finger. Finger had been broken in a fight at King and Main. Colson refuses to provide his address or any further information re. incident. Arrested.
11:30	Transported to station.
11:50am	At stn. Colson processed.
1:20am	Lunch. Relieve driver—Ali.
	Resume duty. GP.
	Check Commissioner re drag races. On loc. observe 2 vehicles from a distance who appear to be speeding and racing side by side. Pursue vehicles. Advise dipatcher re pursuit. Sgt of communications advises—call off pursuit.
2:40am	10-8. GP.
6:30am	Make way to stn re shift change
6:45am	10-7 station
7:00am	Report off Duty
	J. Cartledge P.C. 577
	Sgt. Wickie

■ EXERCISE 6.2   MEMO BOOK ENTRY

1. Watch the video of a crime. Record information that will need to be written in a memo book.

2. Write your memo book entry, providing the necessary details.

EXERCISE

CHAPTER 7
Spelling and Grammar

SPELLING WORD LIST

Following is a reference list of the proper spellings of words commonly used in law enforcement writing.

A

abandon
abbreviation
abdomen
abductor
abet
abortion
abrasion
absence
absolutely
accelerate
acceptance
access
accessory
accidental
accommodate
accomplice
accordance
accost
accuracy
accused
acknowledge
acquaint
acquaintance
acquiesce
acquittal
addressed
adequate

adjourn
adjournment
adjudicated
administrative
admissible
adolescent
adversary
affidavit
affirm
agent
aggravate
agreement
aisle
alcohol
alias
alibi
alien
allege
altercation
alternative
amalgamation
ambiguity
ambiguous
ambulance
amend
ammunition
among

amphetamine
analyze
annual
anonymous
apparatus
apparent
appearance
appellant
apprehend
appropriate
arraignment
arrangement
arrears
arson
artifact
ascertain
asphyxiate
assailant
assassin
assault
assessment
assistant
asthma
attest
attorney
audible
autopsy

B

bail	beginning	boulevard
bailiff	believe	Breathalyzer
balaclava	belligerent	brilliant
ballistics	beneficiary	bruise
bankrupt	benefit	burglarize
barbiturate	bestiality	business
barrel	bias	bystander
barricade	binding	
barrister	bludgeon	

C

cadaver	comatose	consensus
calendar	commission	consequences
calibre	commitment	conspicuous
campaign	committee	conspirator
cancel	compel	contagious
canine	compellable	contemporaneous
capable	competent	contempt
cardiac	complainant	contraband
cartridge	compliance	controversy
casualty	complicity	conviction
category	computer	convulsion
censor	conceive	coroner
changeable	concentrate	corpse
characteristic	conciliation	corroborate
circumstantial	concurrent	counsel
citation	condemn	counterfeit
civilian	condom	courteous
cocaine	conducive	credibility
coerce	confession	cremate
cognizance	confidential	criminal
coincidence	confiscate	criticism
collateral	conscience	culpable
colleague	consciousness	culprit
collision	consecutive	custody

D

damages	deferred	dependent
decapitate	deficient	deposition
deceased	deformities	descend
deceitful	delegate	despair
deceive	deliberate	detain
defendant	delinquent	detention

deterrent
detonator
develop
deviant
diabetes
diagonal
dilapidated
disagreeable
disappointment

discipline
discrepancy
discriminate
disguises
disgusting
disorderly
dispatcher
disperse
disposition

dissatisfied
dissension
dissipate
distress
divulge
dominant
drunkenness
duress
dysfunction

E

electrocution
elicit
eligible
eliminate
elusive
embarrass
embezzle
eminent
enforceable
environment
epileptic
equivalent

erratic
erroneous
espionage
essential
ethical
evidence
exaggerate
excessive
excite
exculpatory
execute
exert

exhaust
exhibit
existence
expiration
explanation
extenuating
external
extinguish
extradite
extraneous
extraordinary
extremely

F

fabricate
facilitate
facility
fallacy
falsify
fatality
fellatio
felon

fictitious
flexible
fluctuate
forceps
forcible
forehead
foreign
forensic

forfeit
forgery
formula
fornicate
fraud
fraudulent
fugitive

G

gambling
garnishee
gauge
genuine

geriatric
graffiti
grievance
grievous

grudge
guarantee
guerrilla
gymnasium

H

habitual	helicopter	hostile
hallucinate	hemorrhage	hurriedly
handcuff	heroin	hygiene
harass	homicidal	hypodermic
hazardous	homicide	hysteria

I

identical	inconspicuous	inquest
identification	incorrigible	insanity
ideology	incriminate	inscribe
illegitimate	inculpatory	insolent
illicit	indecent	inspector
immediate	indelible	institute
immigrant	indictable	insufficient
imminent	indictment	intelligence
impediment	indiscreet	intercede
impostor	inducement	intercourse
inadmissible	inebriated	interpretation
incapable	inevitable	interrogate
incapacitate	infanticide	interview
incarcerate	influential	intoxicated
incendiary	informant	invasion
incentive	infringement	investigator
incessant	ingenious	irrelevant
incestuous	initiate	irresistible
incite	injunction	irresponsible
incoherent	innocent	irritable
incompetent	inoculate	

J–K

jamb	judicial	khaki
jealous	jurisdiction	kidnap
jewelry	juvenile	kleptomaniac
judgment		

L

laboratory	legislate	liaison
laceration	legitimate	lien
larceny	lenient	litigant
latent	liability	lucid

M

magazine
magistrate
malice
malicious
malign
mandatory
manipulate
manoeuvre
marijuana

massacre
median
memorandum
methadone
mileage
militia
miscellaneous
mischievous
mitigating

monotonous
moratorium
morgue
mortgage
mortuary
motorist
mucus
mutilate
muzzle

N

narcotics
necessary
negative
negligence

negotiate
neutral
nominal
notary

notorious
nuisance
nullify

O

obscenity
occasion
occult

occupant
occurrence
omission

ordinance
orthodox

P

parallel
paramedic
paraphernalia
pathologist
pavilion
pedestrian
penetration
penitentiary
permissible
perpetrator
persevere
persistent
personal
personnel
persuade
pertinent

physician
physique
plaintiff
polygraph
pornography
possession
precede
precedent
preliminary
premises
preparation
prescription
prevalent
priority
probable
procedure

proceedings
prohibition
projectile
prominent
promotion
propeller
prophylactic
prosecute
prostitute
protester
provocation
psychiatrist
psychopathic
punitive
pyromaniac

Q

quadrant
quadriplegic
quarantine

quarrel
quash
query

quotation

R

rabies
reasonable
receipt
receptacle
recidivist
recognizance
recognize
recommend
reconcile

reconnaissance
referred
reformatory
refute
regardless
reinforcement
relevant
relinquish
rendezvous

reprieve
rescue
resident
residue
respiration
resuscitate
ricochet
robbery

S

sabotage
sacrifice
scenario
schedule
schizophrenic
seize
senile
sentence
separation
sequence
sergeant
severance
sheriff
siege
significant

silhouette
simultaneous
solicit
solicitor
specimen
spectator
spontaneous
statute
strategy
strenuous
subject
subpoena
substantiate
suffocate
suicide

summarily
superficial
superfluous
superintendent
superintendent
supplementary
surveillance
susceptible
suspect
suspension
suspicious
symmetrical
symptom
syringe

T

tactical
tariff
taut
technique
temperament
tendency

terrorism
testimony
thief
tolerance
tragedy
trajectory

tranquillizer
trauma
treacherous
trespass
truancy

U–V

ultimatum	velocity	victim
unanimous	vengeance	violation
unmistakable	verdict	viscous
	version	volatile
vacuum	vicinity	
vagrant	vicious	

W–Y–Z

waiver	yield	zealous
warrant		
weapon		

WRITING PITFALLS

When writing in your notebooks or when preparing any other documents that may be viewed by others, make sure that you use the correct words and that you spell them correctly. Don't hesitate to refer to a dictionary to check the spelling and meaning of the words you use. See also the preceding word list. Many writers have difficulty with the following words.

accept, except

Accept is a verb meaning "to receive."

She *accepted* the award for Constable of the Year.

Except is most commonly a preposition or conjunction meaning "but," "only," or "other than."

He was on duty every day *except* Thursday.

affect, effect

Affect is a verb meaning "to influence" or "to pretend to have."

The victim's emotional testimony *affected* the jurors' verdict.

Effect is a noun meaning "result."

The victim's testimony had a lasting *effect* on the jurors.

allot, a lot

Allot is a verb meaning "to give or distribute in parts."

We will *allot* each informant a share of the reward.

A lot is two words meaning "much" or "many."

There were *a lot* of witnesses to the crime.

could've, could of
should've, should of
would've, would of

Could've, should've, and **would've** are abbreviations of "could have," should have," and "would have." **Could of, should of,** and **would of** are incorrect grammar and should never be used!

The officer *should've* questioned the witness immediately.

council, counsel

Council is a noun meaning a "group of people who have been elected or appointed to make decisions or laws or to give advice."

At last night's *council* meeting, our police chief requested the budget to hire more officers.

Counsel is a noun meaning "advice" or "lawyer(s)," or a verb meaning "to give advice."

The *counsel* for the defence questioned the officer.

e.g., i.e.

E.g. means "for example."

There are many ways to become physically fit—*e.g.*, walking, running, weight training, and exercising.

I.e. means "that is."

The officer stressed the importance of cooperation—*i.e.*, the need for the public to work with the police to find the thief.

its, it's

Its is the possessive form of "it."

The unit received *its* first 911 call of the week.

It's is the abbreviation of "it is."

It's the first 911 call of the night.

saw, seen

Saw is the past tense of the verb "to see."

> I *saw* the suspect run between the two houses.

Seen is the present perfect tense of the verb "to see," and must be accompanied by helping verbs such as "have" or "has." It is never used alone as the verb in a sentence.

> I *have seen* a suspect pull a knife on an officer.

that, who

That is used for inanimate objects and animals.

> The call *that* came over the radio was for another car.

Who is used for people.

> The man *who* received a ticket was irate.

than, then

Than is a preposition used for comparison.

> He would rather walk a beat *than* give out speeding tickets.

Then is usually an adverb meaning "in the past" or "at a time in the future." It is never a conjunction.

> The speeding car entered a school zone, and *then* I terminated the pursuit.

their, there, they're

Their is the possessive form of "they."

> The officers' shotguns were in *their* trunk.

There is an adverb showing the place of something, or it can be used when the verb comes before the subject in a sentence.

> *There* were 10 officers at the scene.

They're is the contraction of "they are."

> *They're* almost ready to write the GATB test.

were, we're, where

Were is the past tense of the verb "to be."

> The officers *were* in the courthouse.

We're is the contraction of "we are."

> *We're* using dogs to track the missing child.

Where is an adverb or a noun meaning "in, at, or from what place."

> The suspect asked, "*Where* is my lawyer?"

whose, who's	**Whose** is the possessive form of "who."
	The man *whose* car was illegally parked received a ticket.
	Who's is the contraction of "who is."
	Who's the officer in charge this weekend?

THE SENTENCE

1. Avoiding Fragment Sentences

A sentence is a group of words that makes sense on its own. In order for a group of words to be a sentence, or a complete thought, it must contain a subject and a predicate.

It is important that you can identify the subject(s) and verb(s) in your own sentences to ensure that you don't write fragment statements. We often use fragments in conversation because the subject or verb is already understood, or when we take point-form notes because it saves time. In more formal communication, however, fragment sentences are generally not acceptable.

The bare subject usually consists of a noun or a pronoun. Nouns are names of people, places, or things, and pronouns are words such as "I," "you," "he," "she," "we," "it," and "they," which replace nouns. Less well-known pronouns include "anyone," "anybody," "each," "everyone," "everybody," "no one," "nobody," "one," "someone," and "somebody."

The bare predicate consists of a verb, which is most often an action word; a verb may, however, simply link the subject to the predicate.

The subject is usually the person, place, or thing performing the action or being acted upon, and the verb is usually the action performed. Even a simple two-word statement can contain a subject and a verb. For example:

Thieves steal.

Here the subject, "thieves," performs the action, "steal."

In most sentences it is easier to identify the verb first. Usually it is an action word that can be altered or added to, to show a change in time. For example, "steal" is an action word that can be changed to "stole," "have stolen," "will steal," "will have stolen," and so forth, to show a change in time.

Identifying the Action Verb

You can identify the verb by asking yourself, "What is the action that occurs in the sentence?" or "What happened, is happening, or will happen?" In the sentence "Thieves steal," it is "steal."

Identifying the Subject

Once you have located the verb, you can identify the subject by simply asking yourself, "Who or what is performing the action?" In the sentence "Thieves steal," ask "Who or what steals?" It is "thieves."

Even in more complicated statements, there must be a subject and verb. For example:

The three *suspects*, who stand accused of robbing the bank, *were apprehended* after a high-speed chase.

In sentences such as the one above, you may need to ignore some of the distracting details and focus on the action first. Again ask yourself, "What happened?" Notice that the verb here is two words: "were apprehended." Then ask, "Who or what were apprehended?" Here the subject is "suspects."

Commands and Instructions

What appears to be an exception to the rule that every sentence must have a subject and a verb is the giving of a command or instruction. In such instances, the person being spoken to usually knows who he or she is, so a noun or pronoun does not need to be used. It is understood. This is the case, for example, if someone asks you for directions and you reply, "*Turn* left at the first set of lights." The verb is "turn" because it is the action, but here the subject is an understood "you."

Identifying the Linking Verb

Verbs do not always show action. Instead, they may be words that link the subject to the predicate of the sentence. Some linking verbs are:

am	is	are
was	were	seem
appear	feel	grow
become	look	smell
sound	taste	

For example, you can see someone put something into his or her mouth and chew, but you can't actually observe the action of tasting (the chemical reaction).

When a linking verb is used, it is sometimes easier to identify the subject first by asking yourself, "Who or what is the sentence about?" Then locate the verb. For example:

Driving is a privilege.

The sentence is about "driving," which is the subject, and "is" is the verb.

Sometimes a verb can either show action or be a linking verb, depending on how it is used in the sentence. For example, in the first sentence that follows, the verb "appeared" is used to show action, and in the second, "appeared" simply links the subject to the predicate.

The suspect's car *appeared* at the corner.

The victim *appeared* pale as he went into shock.

In the second sentence, we cannot see the chemical and physical reaction that caused the colour change—we only see the result of that reaction.

EXERCISE

■ EXERCISE 7.1   AVOIDING FRAGMENT SENTENCES

Identify which of the following groups of words are fragment sentences by placing an X in the space to the left of each statement. Then underline each subject with one line and each verb with two lines. Correct the fragment sentences by adding the missing subjects or predicates.

_____ **1.** The police protect the public.

_____ **2.** The dogs who cornered the suspect in the neighbours' yard.

_____ **3.** We were present at the inquiry.

_____ **4.** Newfoundland police have only recently been allowed to carry their revolvers.

_____ **5.** An accident occurred at 1800 hours.

_____ **6.** The house invasion was committed while the owners were away on vacation.

_____ **7.** Wait for the light to change.

_____ **8.** The inmates at the city jail rioted.

_____ **9.** During the interrogation, the suspect seemed confident and relaxed.

_____ **10.** Reported the accident by calling 911.

_____ **11.** She will join the canine unit next month.

_____ **12.** By the year 2010, he will have been with the police service for 45 years.

(Exercise 7.1 is continued on the next page.)

(Exercise 7.1 continued ...)

____ **13.** Probing questions were asked by the lawyer for the defence.

____ **14.** There are 60 officers on the local police service.

____ **15.** Do not disturb the crime scene.

____ **16.** The dog picked up the scent of the missing child.

____ **17.** After the robbery, did the first officer on the scene interview the bystanders?

____ **18.** The pedestrian who was hit by the car at the corner of Sanford and Elgin.

____ **19.** The witness testified under oath.

____ **20.** The victim was sent to the hospital for observation.

____ **21.** Some officers dislike giving traffic tickets.

____ **22.** There appeared to be no more witnesses to interview.

____ **23.** Are you patrolling the east side of the city this shift?

____ **24.** After investigating an occurrence, write your report as soon as possible.

____ **25.** Is his partner new in the department?

■ **EXERCISE 7.2   CORRECTING FRAGMENT SENTENCES**

Correct the following fragment sentences by adding the missing subjects or predicates. You may need to add any words that are missing, or delete unnecessary words.

1. The woman accused of abducting the child.

2. Forgot to read the accused his rights.

EXERCISE

(Exercise 7.2 is continued on the next page.)

(Exercise 7.2 continued ...)

3. Pulled the speeding vehicle over and gave the driver a ticket.

4. After the neighbours complained at 2 a.m., the constable who was sent to investigate the noise.

5. The officer's shotgun and ammunition in the trunk of his cruiser, which was parked down the street.

6. The police officer's presentation on teenagers' abuse of alcohol to the Block Parent group who had assembled in the auditorium.

7. When the police officer asked the witness to the assault what she saw, her reply was, "Grabbed hold of the purse, punched the woman in the face, and attempted to run away with the purse in his hand. But two bystanders tackled and held him until you arrived."

8. Women working in non-traditional occupations such as policing and security, which have been thought of as more dangerous jobs held only by men.

(Exercise 7.2 is continued on the next page.)

(Exercise 7.2 continued ...)

9. My appraisal of her progress? Often absent. Handed five assignments in late. Talks incessantly in class.

Rewrite the following paragraph so that it has no fragment sentences. It may be necessary to add or delete words to make the paragraph flow.

10. At 12 p.m. the officers received the call. Respond to a 911 at the corner of East Avenue and Ralph Street. They raced to the scene. Where they found a black male of medium build lying on the sidewalk. His chest covered in blood from what appeared to be a stab wound just below the breastbone. They moved the onlookers back, and called for an ambulance and backup. And, while one checked the victim, the other questioned the bystanders. Three of the people identified the victim's assailant as a white female, 5'6" in height, with blond hair, and wearing blue jeans and a blue jean jacket. Her escape route along Ralph Street into the busy downtown. Disappeared into the crowd.

2. Avoiding Run-On Sentences

A sentence is a group of words that expresses a complete thought. It is important that you use proper conjunctions and avoid the comma splice, so that you can avoid writing run-on sentences.

Identifying Conjunctions

Conjunctions are joining words used to combine two or more sentences. Common conjunctions include "and," "but," "or," "nor," "for," "so," and "yet." Other joining words, used in pairs, include "either/or," "neither/nor," "both/and," and "not only/but also."

Subordinate conjunctions make one part of the sentence appear less important than another. Common subordinate conjunctions are:

after	every time	provided that	until
although	for (because)	rather than	when
as	how	since	whenever
as if	if	so that	where
as long as	inasmuch as	supposing	whereas
as soon as	in case	than	wherever
as though	in order that	that	whether
because	in the event that	the first time	while
before	now that	the last time	who
by the time	once	the next time	why
even if	on condition that	though	
even though	only if	unless	

Note: "Then" is not a conjunction. In the example below, "then" is used incorrectly to join two sentences.

The officer stopped the speeding car, *then* he gave the driver a ticket.

The sentence above may be corrected in a number of ways, as shown below.

The officer stopped the speeding car, *and* then he gave the driver a ticket.

Not only did the officer stop the speeding car, *but* he *also* gave the driver a ticket.

After the officer stopped the speeding car, he gave the driver a ticket.

Avoiding the Comma Splice

The most common run-on sentence written is the comma splice, which occurs when two complete sentences are joined by a comma. For example:

The suspect has dark hair and a moustache, he is approximately 6 ft. (2 m) tall and walks with a slight limp.

There are a number of ways to correct this sentence. One is to divide it into two complete sentences:

The suspect has dark hair and a moustache. *He* is approximately 6 ft. (2 m) and walks with a slight limp.

A second way to correct the sentence is to use a semicolon (;). However, a semicolon should be used only for sentences that are very closely related, and you must be careful not to overuse it.

The suspect has dark hair and a moustache; he is approximately 6 ft. (2 m) tall and walks with a slight limp.

A conjunction can also be used after a semicolon, in which case the conjunction is followed by a comma. Conjunctions that can be used in this way include:

accordingly	generally	moreover	then
also	however	namely	therefore
anyway	incidentally	nevertheless	thus
besides	indeed	normally	undoubtedly
consequently	instead	otherwise	unfortunately
finally	likewise	similarly	
furthermore	meanwhile	still	

With a conjunction and semicolon, the sentence could read:

The suspect has dark hair and a moustache; *furthermore*, he is approximately 6 ft. (2 m) tall and walks with a slight limp.

Notice in the example above that a comma follows "furthermore."

A third way to correct the sentence is to insert a conjunction between the two ideas:

The suspect has dark hair and a moustache, *and* he is approximately 6 ft. (2 m) tall and walks with a slight limp.

A fourth way to correct the sentence is to subordinate one part of the sentence:

The suspect, *who* has dark hair and a moustache, is approximately 6 ft. (2 m) tall and walks with a slight limp.

Notice in the example above that the part of the sentence that is subordinated has a comma before and after it.

If a subordinating conjunction is used at the beginning of the sentence, there must always be a comma after that part of the sentence. For example:

Even though the suspect has dark hair and is 6 ft. (2 m) tall, his moustache and limp are his most distinguishing features.

Avoiding the True Run-On

The true run-on sentence is one that never seems to end. Although conjunctions and punctuation may be used correctly, there are too many ideas in the sentence. For example:

When the officer arrived at the scene of the robbery, he called for backup, but before the other car arrived, he proceeded into the building, where he found the place in shambles and two people gagged and tied together with nylon rope, so he freed them and learned they were the proprietor and her assistant, and that they had been preparing the bank deposit when two males entered the office and robbed them at gunpoint.

The sentence above contains so much information it's hard to keep track of it all, and the reader tends to get lost before he or she finishes reading. By breaking the sentence into shorter bits of information, you can enhance the reader's understanding. When this is done, you may add or delete words to make the sentences flow more smoothly, but be sure you don't omit any necessary information. The maximum number of lines a sentence should cover is three. The following is an example of how the above sentence can be corrected.

When the officer arrived at the scene of the robbery, he called for backup. *Before* the other car arrived, he proceeded into the building, where he found the place in shambles and two people gagged and tied together with nylon rope. *He* freed them and learned they were the proprietor and her assistant. *They* had been preparing the bank deposit when two males entered the office and robbed them at gunpoint.

EXERCISE

■ **EXERCISE 7.3 AVOIDING RUN-ON SENTENCES**

Identify which of the following groups of words are not run-on sentences by placing an X in the space provided to the left of each. Then correct the run-on sentences in the space provided. Try to avoid using the most common conjunctions or the same method of correction for each sentence.

_____ **1.** The city councillors supported community policing, they wanted kiosks set up in all the malls.

_____ **2.** The officer directing traffic appeared to be very warm, I could see the perspiration running down her face.

(Exercise 7.3 is continued on the next page.)

(Exercise 7.3 continued ...)

____ **3.** We completed our investigation of the robbery, then another emergency called us across town.

____ **4.** Last night I walked my beat for five hours without a break because there was a lot of dissension between the residents and the transients who refused to leave the neighbourhood.

____ **5.** While three of the detectives watched from the observation van in case we needed assistance, the rest of us infiltrated the underground organization to find the ring leader and those who protected him as they processed raw heroin, sold it on the street, and then laundered their profits through the electrical business with which they were connected.

____ **6.** There are many good police films made, I wish I could tell which show the officers' actual jobs and which glamourize the position.

(Exercise 7.3 is continued on the next page.)

(Exercise 7.3 continued ...)

_____ **7.** John trained daily; he wanted to be accepted on the tactical squad.

_____ **8.** We questioned the child about his black eye and bruises his reply was hesitant.

_____ **9.** The RIDE officers pulled over 178 vehicles last night 13 drivers had consumed alcohol over the legal limit.

_____ **10.** The community service officer visited four schools during the day, then he attended a home and school meeting that evening.

_____ **11.** The OPP may station their officers anywhere in Ontario, some officers may even be sent to Fort Albany.

_____ **12.** Many people at college tend to forget that a complete education involves both the body and the mind, and in most courses students don't take physical fitness seriously, but those enrolled in the Police Foundations courses must realize how important it is that they be physically fit in order to secure a job once they graduate.

(Exercise 7.3 is continued on the next page.)

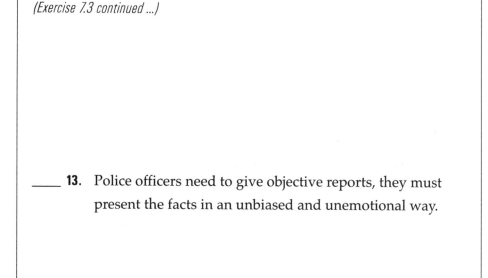

(Exercise 7.3 continued ...)

_____ **13.** Police officers need to give objective reports, they must present the facts in an unbiased and unemotional way.

_____ **14.** At first the officers used shields and batons to protect themselves from the angry protesters, it was finally necessary for the officers to shoot tear gas into the crowd.

Rewrite the following paragraph and punctuate it correctly to eliminate the run-on sentence. It may be necessary to add or delete words to make the paragraph flow.

15. Videotaped and CD-ROM instruction are now available for many subjects, including Police Foundations courses students may sit in front of a television or computer screen and observe lectures, read text, and perform exercises however problems sometimes arise when the students have questions the machines can't answer, there are no professors around to assist them another problem is that the machines can present the theory of, for example, interpersonal communication, without the students actually interacting with another human being, the students can't truly put what they have seen or read into practice and know whether or not their behaviour is acceptable and helpful many feel that machines can easily replace the teacher, isn't the feedback received from others important to police officers whose job it is not only to work with machines, but, more importantly, with the public?

(Exercise 7.3 is continued on the next page.)

(Exercise 7.3 continued ...)

(Exercise 7.3 continued ...)

SIX COMMA RULES

Commas help a sentence to flow smoothly and let the reader know where to pause. Improper comma placement can change the meaning of a sentence and make the sentence difficult to read. Therefore, it is important that you know where and when to use commas.

1. Use a comma before "and," "but," "yet," "for," "so," "or," and "nor" when they connect two complete sentences.

> I wanted to go with them, but I was on duty.

(Note that a comma is placed before "but" because it joins two complete sentences.)

> I wanted to go with them but was on duty.

(Note that no comma is used in this sentence because the words after "but" don't form a complete sentence.)

When a word such as "moreover," "however," "consequently," "nevertheless," "otherwise," "furthermore," "thus," "then," "finally," or "likewise" joins two complete sentences, that word must have a semicolon before it and a comma after it. For example:

> She seemed annoyed; however, she held her temper while she spoke to the rude young offender.

> She seemed annoyed, however, and had difficulty holding her temper while she spoke to the rude young offender.

(Note that in the second sentence, "however" does not join two independent clauses.)

2. Use a comma between items in a series of three or more, and after each part of an address or date.

> He gave his notebook, computer, and incident report to his senior officer.

> She attended report, received her assignment, and began her shift.

(Note the comma before "and" in each of the above examples.)

> The house at 76 Locke Boulevard, in Kingston, was burglarized on Thursday, September 24, of last year.

(Note the commas after both "Kingston" and "24.")

3. Use a comma to indicate a pause after an introductory expression that does not flow smoothly into the sentence or that cannot stand alone as a sentence.

> Unfortunately, I am uncertain whether the suspect had blond or light-brown hair.

> Grabbing her purse, she rushed out the door before the bank robber spotted her.

> After all the neighbourhood watch presentations were assessed, the community representatives voted to introduce the program in their town.

4. Use a comma before and after the name of a person spoken to if the name is in the middle of a sentence. If the name is at the beginning of a sentence, use a comma after it. If it is at the end of a sentence, use a comma before it.

> I recommend, Angela, that you retrace your steps to see what you can remember.

> Angela, I recommend that you retrace your steps to see what you can remember.

> I recommend that you retrace your steps to see what you can remember, Angela.

5. Use a comma before and after an expression that interrupts the flow of a sentence.

> We expect, of course, that you will report on time.

> Mr. Yasas, my neighbour, was involved in a traffic accident last night.

(Note that because "of course" and "my neighbour" could be removed from the above sentences without changing the sentence meaning, commas are placed around these expressions.)

6. Use a comma to separate quotations from the rest of the sentence.

> Sergeant Xiu said, "I need to contact the Toronto Police Services."

(Note that a period is placed inside the quotation mark at the end of the sentence.)

> "I need to contact the Toronto Police Services," said Sergeant Xiu.

(Note that a comma is placed inside the quotation mark even though it is the end of a sentence, where you would normally expect a period. It would not be used if the quotation were a question or exclamation.)

> "I would prefer," said her sergeant, "that you wait to contact them until we receive the results of our own investigation."

(Note that commas are placed around the interrupting phrase "said her sergeant." Note also that the first comma is placed inside the quotation mark.)

Too many commas can clutter a sentence and give it a short, choppy effect; therefore, if you are not sure whether to use a comma, it is often better to leave it out.

■ EXERCISE 7.4   COMMAS AND SEMICOLONS

EXERCISE

In the sentences that follow, place commas and semicolons where they are needed.

1. Although the witness examined the photo lineup three times he could not positively identify the suspect.

2. Constables Lee and Hussein were met at the accident by constables O'Hara Perez and Gauthier.

3. The suspect out-manoeuvred the police officer however he couldn't escape the police dog.

4. In most police service units officers are expected to arrive early for all scheduled meetings.

5. The bystander said "I didn't expect the police to respond so quickly."

6. The suspect was searched handcuffed and helped into the squad car.

7. When they arrived at the station he was booked photographed fingerprinted interrogated and allowed to make a phone call.

8. His lawyer who had bailed him out on several occasions arrived shortly after the suspect was booked.

9. "I'm not sure sir if the fire department will be able to get your cat out of the tree" responded the desk sergeant.

10. Until he was promoted to detective he was just like one of the guys.

11. Habib and Steve both recent Police Foundations graduates have been accepted on the local police service.

12. I wanted to apply for a job with the city police service so I submitted my résumé a cover letter and letters of reference.

13. My credentials were good and my interview went well consequently my name was put on the hiring list.

14. Staff Sergeant Sung the woman who interviewed me assured me that I had a good chance of getting a job.

(Exercise 7.4 is continued on the next page.)

(Exercise 7.4 continued ...)

15. "A witness to the accident Mr. John Henry" said the driver "was standing on the corner."

16. To stay in shape for the fitness exam she runs daily furthermore she works out in the gym three times a week takes aerobics classes and is active on the college swim team.

17. We searched the park the beach and the lakeshore for the missing little boy yet we found no trace of him.

18. By running into the nearest store the woman was able to escape her assailant.

19. Twice he was late arriving for work. We know therefore that he will be put on report.

20. Five bystanders came forward and each had a different description of the car.

THE APOSTROPHE

The correct placement of apostrophes lets the reader identify words that are singular, plural, possessive, or contractions. Improper apostrophe placement can change the meaning of a sentence and make it difficult to understand. Therefore, it is important that you know where and when to use apostrophes.

Showing Possession

When the "s" at the end of a noun is simply used to indicate number (more than one), an apostrophe is not used. However, when you need to show possession (that the noun owns or possesses something), you must use an apostrophe before or after the "s."

Apostrophe Placement for Singular Possessive Nouns

If you have the singular noun, "girl," and the girl has a hat, it is *the girl's hat*. To determine where the apostrophe lies, change the expression around and put "hat" first. In other words, it is *the hat of the girl*. Notice that "girl" here doesn't end in an "s," so the apostrophe is placed between the "l" and the "s." For example:

Singular	Singular possessive
one *boy*	one *boy's* hat

(It is the hat of one boy. Notice that the noun "boy" does not end in an "s.")

Apostrophe Placement for Plural Possessive Nouns

If you have the plural noun "girls," and the girls have hats, they are *the girls' hats*. To determine where the apostrophe lies, change the expression around and put "hats" first. In other words, they are *the hats of the girls*. Notice that "girls" here ends in an "s," so the apostrophe is placed after the "s." For example:

Plural	Plural possessive
six *boys*	six *boys'* hats

(They are the hats of six boys. Notice that the noun "boys" ends in an "s.")

Apostrophe Placement When the Word Form Changes

Sometimes a noun changes in form (from "y" to "ie") when it is made plural. In this case, the plural, the singular possessive, and the plural possessive of this noun all sound alike. Therefore, the use of an apostrophe and its placement shows the difference. For example:

Singular	Plural	Singular possessive	Plural possessive
one *baby*	six *babies*	one *baby's* hat	six *babies'* hats
	(Notice that the noun changes in form.)	(It is the hat of one baby. Notice that the noun "baby" does not end in an "s.")	(They are the hats of six babies. Notice that the noun "babies" ends in an "s.")

Apostrophe Placement When the Word Form and Sound Change

Sometimes a noun changes more drastically in form (for example, "ox" to "oxen") when it is made plural. If the sound of the noun changes when it is made plural, this affects the placement of the apostrophe. For example:

		Singular possessive	Plural possessive
Singular	Plural		
one *man*	six *men*	one *man's* hat	six *men's* hats
	(Notice that the noun changes in both form and sound.)	(It is the hat of one man. Notice that the noun "man" does not end in an "s.")	(They are the hats of six men. Notice that the noun "men" does not end in an "s.")
one *person*	six *people*	one *person's* hat	six *people's* hats
	(Notice that the noun changes in both form and sound.)	(It is the hat of one person. Notice that the noun "person" does not end in an "s.")	(They are the hats of six people. Notice that the noun "people" does not end in an "s.")

It is important to remember that apostrophes are not used with possessive pronouns such as "hers," "his," "its," "ours," and "theirs."

EXERCISE

■ EXERCISE 7.5   USING APOSTROPHES TO SHOW POSSESSION

Correct the sentences below by placing apostrophes where they are needed.

1. The victims testimony was believed by the jurors. *(one victim)*

2. The ladies purses were stolen while they swam.

3. Child care workers must inform the police about childrens suspicious injuries.

4. Officers in-car computers allow them to quickly check peoples records.

5. The narcotics officer relies on his dogs nose to sniff out hidden drugs.

6. Twelve incident reports were recorded in the constables notebook. *(one constable)*

7. In the late afternoon, the womens husbands returned from the weapons inspection.

(Exercise 7.5 is continued on the next page.)

(Exercise 7.5 continued ...)

8. The motorcycle gangs club house was raided by the tactical squads senior officers.

9. The officers demeanour indicated that she wanted the information right away.

10. When they reported the lone assailants appearance, no bystanders description was the same as any others.

11. If it had not been for the junkies assistance, we would not have identified the suspects car. *(one junkie; more than one suspect)*

12. The mountainous terrain made finding the mans wife and child difficult.

13. Tonights weather may hinder our rescue efforts.

14. Her familys concern for her safety stems from her refusal to remove her guard dogs muzzles.

15. Each security officers job is to protect the celebrities during the Academy Awards presentations.

16. The trial judges influence on the jury members was evident.

17. Everybodys opinion of the jurors verdict was different.

18. The criminals hopes sank when he was refused early parole.

19. Some citizens groups believe we should pay more attention to victims rights than to criminals liberty.

20. On my mother-in-laws advice, I applied to work in our police services canine unit.

Forming Contractions

An apostrophe is used when two words are shortened into one, and it is placed where the letter (or letters) is left out. The following is a list of some contractions.

are not = aren't	did not = didn't
cannot = can't	do not = don't
could have = could've	have not = haven't
could not = couldn't	I am = I'm

I had, I would = I'd	they had, they would = they'd
I have = I've	we are = we're
I will, I shall = I'll	we have = we've
is not = isn't	we will = we'll
it is, it has = it's	we had, we would = we'd
it will, it shall = it'll	who will = who'll
she had, she would = she'd	will not = won't*
she is, she has = she's	would have = would've
should not = shouldn't	would not = wouldn't
there is = there's	you are = you're
they are = they're	you will, you shall = you'll
they have = they've	you had, you would = you'd
they will, they shall = they'll	

* Note the change in spelling when "will not" is shortened to "won't." The apostrophe placement is where the last letter, "o," is missing. The same applies to the contraction of "shall not," which is "shan't," although this form is seldom used.

When a letter or number is omitted, as in *o'clock* for *of the clock* or *'98* for *1998*, you add an apostrophe in place of what is omitted. For example:

> I will never forget the crash, at 3 o'clock in the morning, on that day in June '98, when the downstairs window was smashed.

EXERCISE

■ EXERCISE 7.6   FORMING CONTRACTIONS

In the following sentences, make contractions wherever possible. (You may also need to correct errors in possession.)

1. The suspect would not cooperate with the police.

2. I have found that too many people do not obey the rules of the road.

3. The officer said she had requested assistance and could not proceed until more officers arrived.

4. Who has applied for a field placement with the local police service?

(Exercise 7.6 is continued on the next page.)

(Exercise 7.6 continued ...)

5. They have little concern for their dogs safety in most situations, but they should not believe that nothing will ever happen.

6. You are the last person I expected to see drinking and driving!

7. The OPP is not hiring right now; however, that does not mean it will not be looking for cadets in the new year.

8. We have had difficulty getting witnesses to come forward, and I am concerned that we will never be able to identify the hit and run driver.

9. There are not many patrol cars in our neighbourhood because they are needed in other parts of the city.

10. The officer asked the children if they would like to pet his police dog.

Making Plural and Possessive Abbreviations

When abbreviations such as P.C. are made plural, you add an apostrophe before the "s." When lowercase letters such as "p" and "q" are made plural, you add an apostrophe before the "s." For example:

> P.C.'s Evans and Wong were the first officers on the scene.

> Do you remember your mother telling you to mind your p's and q's when you misbehaved?

When abbreviations such as RCMP, OPP, MP, and ABC are possessive, you add an apostrophe before or after the "s," depending on whether the abbreviation is singular or plural. It is important to note that the letters in these abbreviations are not followed by periods. For example:

> The RCMP's duty was to escort the MPs' cars through the city.

In other words, it was the duty of the RCMP (therefore, there is an apostrophe before the "s"), and they were the cars of the MPs (therefore, there is an apostrophe after the "s").

Note that although the abbreviations are written in upper case, the "s" is in lower case.

When abbreviations such as those mentioned above are made plural, you simply add an "s" without an apostrophe (unless a misreading could occur, as in CBS's). For example:

> Three RCMPs joined forces with the local OPPs to track down the missing person.

EXERCISE

■ **EXERCISE 7.7   MAKING PLURAL AND POSSESSIVE ABBREVIATIONS**

Correct the sentences below by placing apostrophes where they are needed.

1. Officers from the OPPs tactical squad requested information from the RCMPs criminal investigation unit.

2. In elementary school we were told to learn our ABCs so that we could write without difficulty when we got older.

3. Some RCMPs worked with the CIAs drug enforcement unit to break the cocaine ring.

4. Students in the Police Foundations Program are often referred to as PFPs.

5. Because they will work with the public, PFPs communication skills must be good.

6. The Ontario PMs office was swarmed by opposition MPs secretaries, and the OPP was called in to escort them out.

7. After WWII, some RCAF officers flew supply missions for the OPPs Northern Ontario Relief Organization.

8. Remember to dot all your is and cross all your ts.

Making Plural and Possessive Numbers

When numbers such as "1999," and "20" are made plural, you simply add an "s" without an apostrophe. (The rule varies on this. Some sources may suggest that you add an apostrophe and an "s.") For example:

> In the *1990s*, the average temperature was in the mid *20s*.

When numbers such as those above are made possessive, you add an apostrophe before or after the "s," depending on whether the number is singular or plural. For example:

> It is understandable that *2002's* police uniforms are different from the less practical *'20s'* attire.

In other words, they are the uniforms of 2002 (therefore, there is an apostrophe before the "s"), and it is the attire of the 1920s (therefore, there is an apostrophe before the "2" and after the "s").

■ EXERCISE 7.8   MAKING PLURAL AND POSSESSIVE NUMBERS

EXERCISE

Correct the sentences below by placing apostrophes where they are needed.

1. During the 1950s housing boom, cities grew, and larger police departments were required.

2. The late 1980s growth in town sizes was reminiscent of the growth of the 1950s.

3. I felt sorry for the traffic officer because the temperature today was in the high 30s, and with the humidity, it soared to the low 40s.

4. The average mark on the entrance exam was in the 80s, but the applicants knew that the year 2004s requirements would dictate that they get in the 90s.

5. Before the 90s switch to coin, our paper currency was in 1s, 2s, 5s, 10s, 20s, 50s, and so on; now we no longer have 1s and 2s.

Making Nouns Ending in "S" Possessive

When a singular noun ends in "s"—for example, "witness" and "Ross"—you write the possessive form with an apostrophe and an "s." (The rule varies on this. Some sources may suggest you add only an "s.") On the other hand, when a plural noun ends in "s," such as "Niagara Falls" (where there is more than one waterfall), "Griggs" (which includes all the family members, each having the last name Grigg), "Joneses" (which includes all the family members, each having the last name Jones), and "witnesses," you simply add an apostrophe and no "s" to show the possessive. For example:

> *Ross's* sister easily slipped out of the *Niagara Falls'* casino and avoided the security guards, because of the sole *witness's* vague description of her.

In other words, it is the sister of the singular "Ross" (therefore, there is an apostrophe followed by an "s"), it is the casino in "Niagara Falls," which is a plural noun (therefore, there is an apostrophe and no "s"), and it is the description of the one "witness" (therefore, there is an apostrophe followed by an "s").

Sergeant *Bliss's* first assignment was to oversee an investigation of a break and enter at the *Franks'* house on Grand Avenue.

In other words, it was the assignment of the singular "Bliss" (therefore, there is an apostrophe followed by an "s"), and it is the house of the Frank family, where all the Franks live (therefore, there is an apostrophe and no "s").

EXERCISE

■ **EXERCISE 7.9   MAKING NOUNS ENDING IN "S" POSSESSIVE**

Correct the sentences below by placing an apostrophe (and perhaps an "s") where needed.

1. Sergeant Gibbins was a veteran investigator for the police service; therefore, when Gibbins staff sergeant gave him traffic duty on a Paris side road, he knew something was wrong.

2. Three officers failed the inspection: Aramass revolver was on the car seat beside him; Harness notebook was not complete; and Thomas reports had not been filed for two weeks.

3. The OPP graduation celebration was held at the Smith Falls community centre.

4. Tess check of the alarm system at the Monsamis house was greatly appreciated by Mr. Monsami because he and his family were leaving on vacation and he wanted to make sure that the alarm was working properly.

5. The witness statement was recorded in Constable Swiss notebook.

6. When the Davises returned home after an evening out and found their front door open and lights on inside, they went to Ms Waters house next door to phone the police.

PARALLEL STRUCTURE

Parallel structure helps you make your message clear. It involves putting similar things in the same form. For example, when you write things in a series, parallel structure makes the information easy to follow and understand. For example:

> The victim was *beaten, stabbed*, and *robbed*.

Note that "beaten," "stabbed," and "robbed" are all written using the same form.

You can check to be sure that you've used parallel structure in the above example because you can say:

◆ The victim was *beaten*.

◆ The victim was *stabbed*.

◆ The victim was *robbed*.

Each of the statements flows smoothly and makes sense.

It takes more concentration on the part of the reader to understand the following example, in which the same form is not used:

> The victim was *beaten, stabbed*, and *then her money was stolen*.

You run into problems when you try to join each action to the first part of this sentence:

◆ The victim was *beaten*.

◆ The victim was *stabbed*.

◆ The victim was *then her money was stolen*.

Note that the last statement doesn't flow smoothly, nor does it make sense. Sentences such as these force the reader to slow down and reread to try to make sense of them.

Following is another example of the need for parallel structure:

> The police did not suspect the young woman because she was tiny, frail, and she looked innocent.

The last part of the sentence isn't parallel with what comes before it, and this can be proven by saying:

◆ The police did not suspect the young woman because she was *tiny*.

◆ The police did not suspect the young woman because she was *frail*.

◆ The police did not suspect the young woman because she was *she looked innocent*.

To correct it, you need to change the last part of the sentence to "innocent looking." The resulting parallel sentence reads:

> The police did not suspect the young woman because she was *tiny, frail*, and *innocent looking*.

It is important to use parallel structure when giving directions. Directions are usually written in the present tense, and are most clearly presented in a list. For example, if a visitor to the city asks an officer to give him directions to the nearest gas station, she may reply as follows:

To get to the Petro Canada station, you

- ◆ *turn* left at the first stoplights you come to, onto Catherine Street;

- ◆ *follow* Catherine through two intersections;

- ◆ *turn* right at the third intersection, onto Henry Avenue;

- ◆ *drive* through six intersections, the last being George Street;

- ◆ *turn* right into the Petro Canada station, in the middle of the next block.

Note that each direction begins with a verb, and each verb is written in the present tense. Also note that information within each direction is presented in the same way. The street names are identified at the end of each direction. This allows the listener to anticipate the information that is coming and the pattern that's being used to present the information; therefore, he or she can easily organize it in his or her mind. (If the officer had said, "turn left at the first stoplights you come to, onto Catherine Street" in the first direction, and "turn right onto Henry Avenue at the third intersection" in the third direction, no pattern would be established, so the listener couldn't anticipate what was coming next.)

EXERCISE

■ EXERCISE 7.10   PARALLEL STRUCTURE CORRECTIONS

In the space provided, correct the errors in parallel structure in the following sentences.

1. The recruit was a tall, handsome athlete and had muscles.

2. Long lectures, difficult books, and writing frequent tests are part of every cadet's life.

(Exercise 7.10 is continued on the next page.)

(Exercise 7.10 continued ...)

3. She liked the sturdiness of the car and how it performed on the road.

4. His argument for free parking was clear, coherent, and it was also passionate.

5. The officer will show you where to go and the turns you should make on the way.

6. To experience job satisfaction is as important as earning money.

7. Pay careful attention to spelling and punctuation and word usage should be checked, too, in your reports.

8. The Willow Tree will either have its alarm system installed on Monday or Tuesday.

9. We left Burtch Correctional Facility at noon and Kingston Penitentiary was arrived at at nine.

(Exercise 7.10 is continued on the next page.)

(Exercise 7.10 continued ...)

10. He wanted to take his stereo system, television, and throw in his Sega games with him to the Milton Correctional Facility.

11. The squeegee kid said he would neither stop interrupting, nor was he going to leave the driver he had been harassing alone with the officer.

12. The elderly man went into great detail about the physical appearance of his assailant and of the curious habit he had of pulling at his ear.

13. I believe the day will come when we will pay at toll booths to drive on highways or having a bill sent to our homes.

14. Mary excels in vehicle training, at the firing range, and while she is studying self-defence.

15. In appearance she was untidy, over-dressed, and with too many jewels.

(Exercise 7.10 is continued on the next page.)

(Exercise 7.10 continued ...)

16. The villagers gave José a perfect description of the two men and that they had started north on foot a week before.

17. I asked the security guards to patrol the beach, mingle in the crowds, and breaking up any disturbances, too.

18. If a car overturned and was burning, and men were being trapped in the vehicle, they could be rescued by passersby.

19. A recruit is expected to come to the examination with a clear head, well prepared, and full of determination to do her best.

20. Teamwork is displayed by a constable who has a great respect for his partner and his actions, and defending him in difficult situations.

AVOIDING WORDINESS AND INFLATED LANGUAGE

It's important that you speak and write to be understood by your audience. Remember that good writing is concise! If you apply the following rules, you should find yourself clearly and successfully presenting your information.

◆ *If you can say something in 5 words, don't say it in 10.* For example, "in this day and age" is better expressed as "today."

◆ *Don't say things twice.* For example, "circled around and around" is better expressed as "circled."

◆ *Eliminate expressions that add nothing to the meaning of the sentence.* For example, "the fact of the matter is that I can't answer your question" is better expressed as "I can't answer your question."

◆ *Don't use words or jargon that can't be easily understood.* Notebook records and reports aren't the place to display your extensive vocabulary. Remember that the general public's reading level is between grades 7 and 10, and you must make your meaning clear to everyone. You need to present your information clearly and simply in as few words as possible. Study the example below and its correction. Which would you prefer to read?

> It is the policy of the department to provide the proper telephonic apparatus to enable each officer to conduct the interdepartmental communication necessary to discharge his or her responsibilities; however, it is contrary to department regulations to permit telephones to be utilized for personal officer communications.

> *Correction*

> Officers' telephones are provided for department business. It is against department policy to use them for personal calls.

Notice how much easier the correction is to read and understand. It has even been divided into two sentences, which further clarifies the message.

◆ *Exercise judgement!* Don't eliminate words that are needed to make your meaning clear and don't omit words that are needed for the sake of courtesy.

■ **EXERCISE 7.11   ELIMINATING WORDINESS 1**

EXERCISE

Change the bold-faced wordy writing to concise writing.

1. The stain on your shirt is **not visible to the eye**.

2. The victim liked the officer **for the reason that** she was helpful.

3. The Toronto Police Service's uniform is **along the lines of** Hamilton's.

4. Your traffic ticket **is in the amount** of $260.

5. **Due to the fact that** there was a robbery, the officers rushed to the scene.

6. The canine unit will arrive **at a later date**.

7. **Until such time as** the ambulance arrived, the constable performed CPR.

8. The officer repeated his instructions **again and again**.

(Exercise 7.11 is continued on the next page.)

(Exercise 7.11 continued ...)

9. **Enclosed herewith** is my application for employment with your department.

10. He was a cadet **for the duration of** six months.

11. **Will you be so kind as to** answer a few questions. *(Note the end punctuation.)*

12. **There is no doubt but that** you've heard the news about the drug bust.

13. The suspect said to the constable, "I don't have an answer **at this point in time.**"

14. **In the event that** the GATB test is fair, I'll do well.

15. I'm writing **with reference to** your request for a community home safety presentation.

■ **EXERCISE 7.12   ELIMINATING WORDINESS 2**

EXERCISE

Change the bold-faced wordy writing to concise writing.

1. During the chase, the suspects drove their car into a pond. **At that point in time** their car stalled, and the suspects ran into the woods.

2. **He is an officer who** strives to stay in touch with the public.

3. **A person who is honest** is usually not arrested.

4. **There are some people who** would rather rob a bank than work for minimum wage.

5. When I arrived at the crime scene, **she was there in person.**

6. **Personally, I don't think** the witness has told us all she knows.

7. **My sergeant, she** is always helpful.

8. When we arrived at the gang fight, we were **surrounded on all sides**.

(Exercise 7.12 is continued on the next page.)

(Exercise 7.12 continued ...)

9. The constable received a **free gift** from his sergeant.

10. The suspect's hair is **long in length**; in fact, it hangs past his shoulders.

11. The officer asked the judge if he could **refer back** to his notebook to refresh his memory.

12. The constable said to the victim, "Would you please **repeat again** what you said."

13. There were **two different kinds** of weapons used in the robbery.

14. The cadets received a **free, complimentary copy** of the *Highway Traffic Act*.

15. **During the winter months** officers may be chilled to the bone while on traffic duty.

16. The **very unique** vase has been missing since the robbery.

(Exercise 7.12 is continued on the next page.)

(Exercise 7.12 continued ...)

17. The police informant's **past history** warned the sergeant not to trust her.

18. The **end result** of the investigation was that a suspect was arrested.

19. When we wrote the GATB test, we took pens, pencils, paper, **and et cetera** with us.

20. The thugs' **usual custom** was to don balaclavas before invading people's homes.

■ **EXERCISE 7.13 ELIMINATING WORDINESS AND AVOIDING INFLATED LANGUAGE**

Read the passage below. Rewrite the passage in the space provided and do the following:

1. Locate and change the inflated writing to straightforward, easily understood writing.

2. Locate and eliminate the wordiness.

> The officer officiously strode toward the speeder's automobile. The driver painstakingly scrolled the window down and gazed magnanimously at the officer, inquiring, "For what purpose have you arrested my progress by causing me to move onto the edge of the road and cease my forward movement?"

(Exercise 7.13 is continued on the next page.)

EXERCISE

(Exercise 7.13 continued ...)

The officer, in a deep, guttural voice, asked, "Are you knowledgeable, ma'am, of your incognizant usage of the Queen's highway?"

She replied, "Why, officer, I am flabbergasted that you terminated my motor vehicle experience to query my driving. My driving is innocuous!"

The officer replied, "To me, ma'am, your driving displayed a semblance of undue care and attention for other drivers manipulating their conveyances on the roadway. To wit, you were exhibiting careless driving. Subsequently, I am forthwith going to charge you with this provincial statute offence, which will necessitate your participation in the judiciary process."

SUBJECT–VERB AGREEMENT

A verb must agree with its subject in number. Therefore, the rule is simple. A singular subject takes a singular verb and a plural subject takes a plural verb.

Subjects Not in Prepositional Phrases

Words that come between the subject and verb do not change the subject–verb agreement. If you need to, cross out the prepositional phrases to help you find the subject and verb. For example:

> One ~~of the crooked politicians~~ *was jailed* for a month.

In the above example, the subject looks plural if you think it's "politicians" and don't realize it's in a phrase. By eliminating the phrase, you can see that the subject is actually singular ("one") and requires a singular verb such as "was jailed."

■ **EXERCISE 7.14   SUBJECTS NOT IN PREPOSITIONAL PHRASES**

EXERCISE

Make the subjects and verbs agree in the following sentences by circling the correct verb form for each sentence. (You may cross out phrases.)

1. My sergeant, as well as my partner, (has / have) accompanied me on patrol.

2. Although many people witnessed the accident, only one of the 12 (was / were) able to give me a detailed description of what happened.

3. My family and home life, not to mention my recreational time, (suffers / suffer) when I work the night shift.

4. The desk sergeant, along with those in mobile units, (needs / need) to understand computer fundamentals.

5. All our duties, including report writing, (is / are) important.

6. An officer who walks the beat, as well as those who patrol the suburbs in cars, (records / record) daily occurrences in a notebook.

(Exercise 7.14 is continued on the next page.)

(Exercise 7.14 continued ...)

7. A detective and a forensic officer (was / were) present at the scene.

8. My spouse, as well as my superiors, (wants / want) me to apply for the canine unit.

9. The repeat offender, in accordance with the advice of his counsellors, (has / have) enrolled in an anger management program.

10. The 12 jurors, one of whom believes in the accused's innocence, (remains / remain) locked in deliberation.

Verbs Coming Before Subjects

A verb agrees with its subject even when the verb comes before the subject. Words that may precede the subject include "there," "here," and, in questions, "who," "which," "what," and "where." For example:

Inside the storage shed **are** the garden *tools*.

There **are** *times* I'm ready to quit my job.

Where **are** the *instructions* for this text?

E X E R C I S E

■ EXERCISE 7.15   VERBS COMING BEFORE SUBJECTS

Make the subjects and verbs agree in the following sentences by circling the correct verb form for each sentence. (You may cross out phrases.)

1. When (does / do) you meet with the Block Parent group?

2. In the middle of the field (stands / stand) the memorials to officers killed in the line of duty.

3. There (is / are) an unsigned report on the sergeant's desk.

4. Which (was / were) the bystander's statement recorded by you?

(Exercise 7.15 is continued on the next page.)

(Exercise 7.15 continued ...)

5. Over the fence (scrambles / scramble) the suspects, with the police right behind them.

6. Of all the women in the lineup, which (appears / appear) to be the one you saw running away from the burning building?

7. Whom (has / have) the RCMP investigated concerning the stock fraud?

8. There (is / are) many reasons why the RIDE program should remain in effect.

9. In the trunk of the patrol car (is / are) the officers' shotguns.

10. (Does / Do) the witness have any further information?

Agreement of Indefinite Pronouns and Verbs

Indefinite pronouns such as the following always take singular verbs.

"-one" words	"-body" words	"-thing" words	other words
one	nobody	nothing	each
anyone	anybody	anything	either
everyone	everybody	everything	neither
someone	somebody	something	

Anyone with information about the accident *should contact* the local police.

Everybody in the department *is going* to Sergeant Xiu's retirement dinner.

Something made the customs officer ask to look in the motorist's trunk.

Neither of the corrections officers *was* asked to attend the parole hearing.

EXERCISE

In the following sentences, make the subjects and verbs agree by circling the correct verb form for each sentence. (You may cross out phrases.)

1. Each of the suspects (has / have) red hair.

2. There (is / are) someone patrolling this part of the city every evening.

3. Everything we know about the sniper, including his last known address, (has / have) been published in the newspaper.

4. Nobody (seems / seem) concerned about the break-and-enters during the Christmas season.

5. The 911 caller said, "Someone (needs / need) to send a fire truck. One of my cats (was / were) chased up a tree, and it can't get down."

Agreement of Compound Subjects and Verbs

Compound subjects usually take a plural verb when the subjects are joined by "and." For example:

> *Ambition* and *good luck* **are** the keys to his success.

When subjects are joined by "or," "either ... or," "neither ... nor," "not only ... but also," the verb agrees with the closest subject. For example:

> Either *the canine unit* or *six officers* **were** called to the scene.

> Either *six officers* or *the canine unit* **was** called to the scene.

■ EXERCISE 7.17 AGREEMENT OF COMPOUND SUBJECTS AND VERBS

EXERCISE

In the following sentences, make the subjects and verbs agree by circling the correct verb form for each sentence. (You may cross out phrases.)

1. Both the officers and the suspect (was / were) covered in mud after running through the swamp.

2. Neither the victim nor his assailants (is / are) willing to tell us what started the fight.

3. I don't know if either the Block Parent groups or the Street Proofing Association (receives / receive) community funding.

4. The security officers or the head of mall security (goes / go) to high schools and (talks / talk) to students about the penalties for shoplifting.

5. Not only American cigarettes, but also contraband liquor, (has / have) been smuggled across the border into Canada.

6. The tracking dog and its handler (was / were) commended for finding the lost child.

7. Either the complainant or the accused (is / are) lying.

8. Not only the counsel for the defence, but also the defendants, (seems / seem) nervous about the outcome of the trial.

9. Constable Perez or others from her unit (rides / ride) through the park every day.

10. At night, children and adults alike (is / are) at risk in certain parts of the city.

FAULTY MODIFIERS

A modifier is a word, phrase, or clause that gives more information about another word.

Misplaced Modifiers

In order to be understood correctly, a modifier should be placed as close as possible to the word it modifies. Notice in the examples below how the placement of the modifier "only" affects the meaning of the sentence.

The accused told his lawyer what *only* he had done.

(No one else did it.)

The accused told his lawyer *only* what he had done.

(He didn't tell his lawyer anything else.)

The accused told *only* his lawyer what he had done.

(He didn't tell anyone other than his lawyer.)

Only the accused told his lawyer what he had done.

(No one else told his lawyer.)

Note that in the above examples, "only" precedes the word or words it modifies. When using words such as "only," "almost," "even," "hardly," "just," "merely," and "nearly," be sure to place them right before the words they describe.

Sometimes modifiers are group of words called clauses or prepositional phrases. Usually, when a clause or phrase is misplaced in the sentence, the error is more obvious to the reader. For example, a modifying clause is misplaced in the following sentence.

The dog bit the child on the face, *which was vicious*.

(This phrasing suggests that "face" was vicious because it is the closest noun/pronoun to the clause.)

Written correctly, the above sentence is:

The dog, *which was vicious*, bit the child on the face.

OR

The *vicious dog* bit the child on the face.

In the next example, a modifying phrase is misplaced.

In the holding cell at the city jail, I saw three robbery suspects.

(This suggests that "I" was in the holding cell because it is the closest noun/pronoun not in a prepositional phrase.)

Written correctly, the above sentence is:

At the city jail, I saw three robbery suspects *in the holding cell*.

The sentence below has a misplaced modifier.

The officers patrolled the park *that rode bicycles.*

When this sentence is corrected, the wording changes slightly so that the modifier agrees with the word it describes:

The officers, **who** *rode bicycles,* patrolled the park.

OR

The officers **who** *patrolled the park* rode bicycles.

■ **EXERCISE 7.18   MISPLACED MODIFIERS**

EXERCISE

The following sentences contain misplaced modifiers. In the space provided, correct them by moving each modifier to a more appropriate place in the sentence. You may need to slightly change the wording.

1. At the age of 65, the young constable attended a party for the chief of police, who was retiring.

2. The suspect was running along an alley that was from Thunder Bay.

3. We saw the car strike the telephone pole from our window.

4. The officer drove the patrol car down the city street with his partner that had not been plowed.

(Exercise 7.18 is continued on the next page.)

(Exercise 7.18 continued ...)

5. The informant gives us information often.

6. The detective approached the suspect's house with care.

7. When the woman accused her boyfriend of infidelity, she hardly could contain her anger.

8. The thieves stole all her stereo equipment that broke in through the window.

9. The newspaper photographer showed the robbery pictures to the police officer that he had shot.

10. Community policing involves merely being visible as a helping part of the community and not as law enforcers only. *(Hint: Generally, community policing involves 50 percent community service and 50 percent law enforcement.)*

(Exercise 7.18 is continued on the next page.)

(Exercise 7.18 continued ...)

11. My sergeant told me they needed someone who could translate Cantonese badly.

12. She bought a coffee for her partner that cost $1.25, and he almost drank the whole thing in one gulp.

13. Wearing a blue coat and running shoes, the dog searched for the missing child.

14. The Crown attorney just had left when the jurors returned with their verdict.

15. So that they are deterred from becoming repeat offenders, parole officers should be aware of the location and activities of their clients.

16. The undercover narcotics officer described the smuggler as a tall, white American in a fancy boat with gray hair.

(Exercise 7.18 is continued on the next page.)

(Exercise 7.18 continued ...)

17. The police service nearly serves two million people in this area.

18. Constable Longboat responded in the middle of her shift to a public disturbance call.

19. Driving through blinding snow on an icy road, the accident involved three cars.

20. The surveillance crew watched the drug dealer sell cocaine to school children in their unmarked van.

Dangling Modifiers

Sometimes it isn't clear which word a modifier is describing. Often when this happens in speech, we overlook the error because we are involved in the conversation and understand. In writing, however, the error is more confusing for the reader. To correct dangling modifiers, you can usually add a word for the modifier to describe. For example, a modifier is dangling in the following sentence.

> While watching the security officers chase the fleet-footed suspect, it was hard to believe they would ever catch him.

(This phrasing suggests that "it" watched the security officers chase the suspect because "it" is the closest noun/pronoun.)

Written correctly, the above sentence is:

> While watching the security officers chase the fleet-footed suspect, I found it hard to believe they would ever catch him.

OR

While I watched the security officers chase the fleet-footed suspect, I found it hard to believe they would ever catch him.

Notice that in both the corrections above, some words in the sentence had to be changed.

EXERCISE

■ **EXERCISE 7.19   DANGLING MODIFIERS**

In the space provided, correct the following sentences, which contain dangling modifiers. You will need to change the subject to one the modifier can appropriately describe.

1. Training for the fitness exam, a universal weight fell and narrowly missed my knee.

2. While driving to the scene of an accident, the dispatcher gave us the details.

3. The public service officers found the Block Parent meeting room walking down the hall.

4. After arresting a suspect, the rights to counsel from the *Charter of Rights and Freedoms* should be read.

5. We answered the B & E call, but, upon entering the building, there was no one to be found.

(Exercise 7.19 is continued on the next page.)

(Exercise 7.19 continued ...)

6. Before leaving after your shift, your reports should be completed in full.

7. Speaking to a public school about street proofing, a grade 5 boy asked about bullying.

8. While driving through an intersection on a green light, a blue Chevrolet ran the red and hit my car on the passenger side.

9. Most of the cross-border shopper's purchases, after paying almost $250 for them, were confiscated crossing the border.

10. After rioting in the prison, the guards locked the inmates in their cells.

11. Pursuing the speeding car, the siren was turned on.

(Exercise 7.19 is continued on the next page.)

(Exercise 7.19 continued ...)

12. Determined to catch the Mafia boss, a surveillance was started.

13. As a traffic officer, unobservant drivers are a hazard.

14. In an attempt to relate to community youth, a basketball game was planned.

15. While on duty last night, it rained.

16. On trial for manslaughter, the jurors found him guilty.

17. After watching the woman empty her ashtray on the roadside, she was given a ticket for littering.

18. Since the accused broke the conditions of his bail, an arrest was made.

(Exercise 7.19 is continued on the next page.)

(Exercise 7.19 continued ...)

19. By reporting the vandalism in progress, the Neighbourhood Watch program proved to be invaluable.

20. Locking the shotgun in the trunk of the patrol car, it was out of sight of any bystanders.

THE PAST TENSE

Since law enforcement officers write in their memo books and do their report writing after something has occurred, most of their writing is in the past tense. There are four forms of the past tense from which others are derived. The forms are the simple past, the past progressive, the past perfect, and the past perfect progressive tenses. The exercises in this section involve editing passages. This is what you must be prepared to do with your own work so that it is error-free.

Simple Past Tense

In the simple past tense, the main verb usually ends in "ed." Some verbs, however, are irregular and do not form the past tense by adding "ed." In either case, there are no helping verbs. For example:

The thieves *robbed* the jewelry store during rush hour.

The canine unit *located* the missing child four hours after she disappeared.

I *slept* in and had to hurry to get to work on time.

The stabbing victim *bled* profusely.

■ EXERCISE 7.20   SIMPLE PAST TENSE

The following passage is written in the present tense. Change the verbs to the simple past tense.

E X E R C I S E

> At 10 p.m., P.C. Lee and P.C. Roanski receive a 911, possible stabbing, call at 123 Howard Street. When the officers arrive, P.C. Lee and P.C. Roanski find the victim on the pavement in a pool of blood, with what appears to be a stab wound in his left side. The ambulance is already there, and the attendants say they want P.C. Lee and P.C. Roanski's OK to move him. A group of inquisitive bystanders watch as P.C. Lee secures the area and P.C. Roanski asks for information.
>
> Only one onlooker says he has information. He sees the victim and another person as they come out of the bar across the street. Their loud voices catch his attention as they argue. Then the victim shoves the other person, and, after another loud exchange and more aggressive pushing, the victim falls to the ground. The other person stares at the victim for what seems like a minute, and then runs east down Howard Street toward downtown.

Past Progressive Tense

In the past progressive tense, the main verb ends in "ing," and "was" or "were" is the helping verb. For example:

The driver ***was*** *speeding* when he passed me.

It began to get dark as the officers ***were*** *directing* traffic around the accident.

While some of us ***were*** *writing* the GATB test, others ***were*** *attending* an information session.

Two guards ***were*** *preparing* the prisoner for transport while another ***was*** *bringing* the van to the door.

■ EXERCISE 7.21 PAST PROGRESSIVE AND SIMPLE PAST TENSES

Correct the verbs in the following passage. Try to use the past progressive first and then, as a last resort, the simple past tense. (There are 12 places to use the past progressive tense.)

As a woman crosses the border from the United States into Canada, she stops at the Customs booth. The Customs officer asks her citizenship. When she replies that she is American, the Customs officer asks her where she is from, what her destination is, and how long she intends to be in Canada. She says she is from Chicago and that she is going to meet her elderly relatives who move to Owen Sound in a couple of days. She wants to arrive there before them as a surprise, and to stay with them for a week or two to help them unpack.

While the woman speaks, the Customs officer looks in her car. All of her possessions seem to be in the interior. To him, it looks as though the woman's planning to spend longer than a couple of weeks in Canada, and something isn't right with her story. He asks her to wait for a moment and refers to his notes.

While he checks the most recent bulletins, the woman speeds off. Then he knows for sure something is wrong. The Customs officer immediately calls for assistance, and the police pursue her within minutes.

He's wise to ask for assistance. The woman is a wanted felon and isn't intending to visit anyone. She's simply planning to hide in Canada. Also, she's carrying a loaded revolver, which she uses to rob a convenience store the night before. The police tell him that the woman confesses that she's going to threaten him with the gun if he questions her further.

Past Perfect Tense

In the past perfect tense, the main verb usually ends in "ed," and "had" is the helping verb. For example:

> By the time the detectives looked at the DNA evidence, the forensic team **had** already *examin**ed*** it.

> The officers located the narcotics in the false-bottomed suitcase because they **had** *received* a tip.

> My partner **had left** before I finished my report.

> The security officer **had seen** three unauthorized people enter the building, so he phoned his superior to let him know.

■ **EXERCISE 7.22   PAST PERFECT, PAST PROGRESSIVE, AND SIMPLE PAST TENSES**

EXERCISE

Correct the verbs in the following passage. Try to use the past perfect, then the past progressive, and finally, as a last resort, the simple past tense. (There are 9 places to use the past perfect tense and 4 places to use the past progressive tense.) The verbs to change in the passage are shown in bold-face type.

The jail guard **was seeing** the inmates angry before, but never **has** he **experiences** anything like this. They **yell** and **throw** things against the bars of their cells. It **is** **frightening** for the young guard because he **hears** that this **is** the first sign of a prison uprising.

He **makes** sure he securely **locks** his cell block and **goes** to his supervisor's office. There he **reports** what the inmates **are doing** to their living quarters. The supervisor **asks** if he **knows** what **causes** the problem and if he **is** **trying** to calm the men under his care. The guard **thinks** he **has heard** one man threaten another, but that **is** not unusual. Then he **remembers** that he and some other guards **break** up a vicious fight earlier that day. It **concerns** the turf of two antagonistic groups. That, he realized, **causes** the near-riot in his cell block.

Past Perfect Progressive Tense

In the past perfect progressive tense, the main verb ends in "ing," and "had" is the helping verb along with "been." For example:

> By the time John arrived back at the group home, his supervisor **had been** *looking* for him for two hours.

> It was 1:00 a.m., and the youths **had been** *partying* loudly until the police officer informed them that the noise curfew was 11:00 p.m.

EXERCISE

■ EXERCISE 7.23 USING ALL FOUR VERB TENSES

Correct the verbs in the following passage. Try to use the past perfect progressive as often as possible, then the past perfect, the past progressive, and finally, as a last resort, the simple past tense. (There are 6 places to use the past perfect progressive tense, 6 places to use the past perfect tense, and 7 places to use the past progressive tense.) The verbs to change in the passage are shown in bold-face type.

> From their van, the surveillance team **watches** the house for hours and **seen** nothing. They **are** even **considering** quitting for the day and one officer **gets** ready to pack his equipment away. Suddenly, the man **walks** out of his house. The team in the van **haven't expect** this, so they **have** to scramble to get ready.
>
> The man **carries** a pail and a car wash brush and **tugs** on a hose as he **approaches** his car, which he **is** obviously **prepared** to wash. For an hour, the surveillance team **photograph** his every move as he **fills** the pail, **bends** over and **dips** the brush in the sudsy water, and **proceeds** to scrub his car. They **have been in wait** for an opportunity like this to catch him in the act.
>
> When they **take** enough pictures, the team leader, wearing a wire, **leaves** the van and **approaches** the man. She **asks** him if washing his car **is relaxing** for him, and he eagerly **responds** in the affirmative. Then she **asks** if he **notices** that his muffler **dangles**. He **says** he **knows**, and that he **has** just **planned** to repair it himself but **wants** the driveway to dry first. He even **leans** under the car to point out the damaged area.

(Exercise 7.23 is continued on the next page.)

(Exercise 7.23 continued ...)

Now the team leader **knows** she **has** enough evidence. The surveillance team **photograph** the man's every move, and they **tape** her conversation with him. As she **walks** away, a sly smile **is** even **beginning** to cross her face. The man they **watch** can now be charged with insurance fraud. His severe back injury **isn't** as debilitating as he **claims**.

USING CAPITAL LETTERS

There are six rules to remember when you use capital letters. You must remember to capitalize

1. the first letter of the first word of every sentence;

2. names of people, nationalities, languages, and places;

3. names of particular people or things;

4. names of weekdays, months, and holidays;

5. the first letter of every sentence within a direct quotation; and

6. the first word and all other important words in a title.

1. Capitalize the First Letter of the First Word of Every Sentence

Every new sentence begins with a capital letter. There are no exceptions!

2. Capitalize the Names of People, Nationalities, Languages, and Places

a. Capitalize the Names of People

The first letter of a person's name is always capitalized. This includes any nicknames, given names, and the person's family name. For example: Red, Xiu, Quan, and Stephen Theodore Bruckmann.

b. Capitalize the Names of Nationalities

The nationality of a person always begins with a capital letter. For example: Canadian, Indian, Scandinavian, English, Japanese, and Portuguese.

c. Capitalize the Names of Languages

The name of a language always begins with a capital letter. For example: English, Cantonese, Russian, German, and Spanish.

d. Capitalize the Names of Places

The names of places always begin with a capital letter. For example: Port Elgin, Russell Day Nursery School, Rousseau Street, South America, and the Canadian North.

Note that "north," "south," "east," and "west" are not capitalized when they refer to a direction. They are capitalized only if they refer to a specific place.

3. Capitalize Names of Particular People or Things

The title of a person, if it precedes his or her name, always begins with a capital letter. For example: Aunt Georgina, Doctor Paterson, Sergeant Thomas, Queen Elizabeth, and Professor Bolgan.

If the title is used without the person's name and is preceded by a pronoun, don't capitalize the title. For example: my mother, your brother-in-law, her uncle.

The title of a person, if it replaces the person's name, always begins with a capital letter. For example: Grandpa, Uncle, Officer, Prime Minister, Lieutenant Governor.

Names of pets always begin with a capital letter. For example: Rover, Lucky.

Also, the names given to inanimate objects always begin with a capital letter. For example, you may call your car Bessy or Rust Bucket.

4. Capitalize the Names of Weekdays, Months, and Holidays

The days of the week and the months of the year always begin with a capital letter. For example: Saturday, August.

Names of the seasons are not capitalized. For example: winter, spring, summer, fall.

Special-event days and holidays always begin with a capital letter. For example: Remembrance Day, Easter, Rosh Hashanah, Ramadan.

5. Capitalize the First Letter of All Sentences Within a Direct Quotation

The first letter of any new sentence within a quotation always begins with a capital letter. For example:

The accused demanded, "*Let* me see my lawyer right now!"

"*Let* me see my lawyer right now!" the accused demanded.

"*The* information you want," said the accused, "has nothing to do with me."

6. Capitalize the First Word in a Title and All Other Important Words

All of the important words in titles begin with capital letters. Articles, conjunctions, and prepositions aren't capitalized unless they are the first or last word in the title, or are over four letters long. For example:

Diversity Issues in Policing

The Cobourg Star

Challenge and Survival

An Introduction to Law

This Rock Within the Sea

Setting Out

■ EXERCISE 7.24   USING CAPITALS CORRECTLY

In the sentences below, underline the letters that should be capitalized.

1. sometimes it is impossible to tell the criminal from the victim.

2. the young offender was attending ancaster high and vocational school when he was arrested by officer chen for drug trafficking.

3. the young constable's grandmother always had confidence in his ability to succeed as a law enforcement officer.

4. so that he could attend the hanukkah celebrations in kingston with his family, constable bromberg asked for vacation time in december.

5. the best narcotics sniffer in the canine unit is stop gap, the german shepherd handled by sergeant perez.

6. many chinese-, indian-, and spanish-speaking people are now applying for law enforcement positions in this area.

(Exercise 7.24 is continued on the next page.)

(Exercise 7.24 continued ...)

7. when the president of the united states recently visited canada, the rcmp was on full alert.

8. the book entitled *a report writing guide for the law enforcement profession* will soon be a mandatory resource for all officers.

9. the officer asked, "were you able to see your assailant, mr. wilke?"

   "it was impossible for me to see who attacked me," the victim replied, " because i was jumped from behind."

   "do you remember, when he demanded your wallet, if he had an accent?" asked the officer.

   "it sounded scottish, welsh, or irish, or something like that. i know it wasn't a norwegian accent," answered the victim.

   (Note that when a new person begins to speak, a new paragraph begins.)

10. we tracked the suspect as she drove south to lake ontario and then took the 401 east toward the eastern townships of quebec.

EXERCISE

■ EXERCISE 7.25   EDITING—A GRAMMAR AND SPELLING REVIEW

The following passage contains errors in spelling and in all areas of grammar discussed in this text:

◆ sentence fragments

◆ run-on sentences

◆ commas

◆ apostrophes

◆ parallel structure

◆ wordiness

◆ inflated language

◆ subject–verb agreement

◆ faulty modifiers

◆ past tense

(Exercise 7.25 is continued on the next page.)

(Exercise 7.25 continued ...)

There are 8 spelling errors and 43 grammar errors in the passage below. Edit the passage, correcting the errors.

The R.C.M.P.s' Officer LeDuc is being talked about since her vacation last summer. She rented a cabin in the Northern part of the province, near Moose River, for a vacation. She wanted to get away from the busy city and just relax, but what began as a quiet holiday soon became more exciting than she had wished.

After a few days at the cabin, Officer LeDuc drove into town to look around. She stopped at a variety store for some chocolate bars, and, as she was leaving the parking lot, she seen three people run out of the local bank wearing balaclavas and carrying shotguns and bulky sacks. They jumped into a black Ford van and sped off as people ran out of the bank yelling that they've been robbed and pointing in the direction the van had gone.

She phoned the local constabulary from her car, but their nearest patrol car was 50 kilometres away. Because she was off duty and; therefore, unequipped to handle the situation, her only choice was to follow the fugatives until the local police could catch up.

Officer LeDuc stayed well back from the van, and the occupents didn't seem to notice she was following them. They followed the highway South about 15 kilometres, then they turned onto Little Point Road, a narrow dirt side road, posted with a "Boat Launch" sign. This worried Officer LeDuc, since she was'nt sure of the territory, and knew she was outnumbered. However she also knew the road led to the water, a perfect escape route for the robery suspects as she turned down the road after them, she was glad she's stayed in constant touch with the local dispatcher.

Knowing she had no time to waste, Officer LeDuc sped down the dirt road. Up hills and around sharp bends, until she could see the dust created by the van in front of her. Soon she realized she was right, at the end of the road, a

(Exercise 7.25 is continued on the next page.)

(Exercise 7.24 continued ...)

boat was docked at the East side of a pier. The boat was untied the motor was running and the driver who saw Officer LeDucs car racing toward them motioned to the people in the van to hurry.

Officer LeDuc was close enough to see that the three suspects, now without their balaclavas', were men but she couldn't get to the pier fast enough to prevent them from getting into the boat. She could tell though that they left the van in such haste that they had only taken the sacks, and left all their parephanalia in the van. Although she was a distance away, she must have frightened the suspects as she lept from her car because, to get away, the driver gunned the motor and it stalled.

He tried, and tried, and tried to restart the motor, but to no avail. In the distance, Officer LeDuc could hear the approaching sirens of the local police. Knowing she had to do something to stop the suspects, she siezed a chocolate bar from her car seat. Using her door as a shield, she pointed it at the suspects', identified herself as a Police Officer, and ordered them to put their hands in the air. To her surprise they complied. She was able to detane them until her backup arrive, and they took the men into custody.

From that day forward, Officer LeDuc is known as the candy bar Constable, for her very unique arrest.

Answers for Chapter 7 Exercises

THE SENTENCE

Exercise 7.1   Avoiding Fragment Sentences

_____ **1.** The police protect the public.

__X__ **2.** The dogs cornered the suspect in the neighbours' yard. (This correction is a suggestion only.)

_____ **3.** We were present at the inquiry.

_____ **4.** Newfoundland police have only recently been allowed to carry their revolvers.

_____ **5.** An accident occurred at 1800 hours.

_____ **6.** The house invasion was committed while the owners were away on vacation.

_____ **7.** Wait for the light to change. (The subject _you_ is understood.)

_____ **8.** The inmates at the city jail rioted.

_____ **9.** During the interrogation, the suspect seemed confident and relaxed.

__X__ **10.** We reported the accident by calling 911. (This correction is a suggestion only.)

_____ **11.** She will join the canine unit next month.

_____ **12.** By the year 2010, he will have been with the police service for 45 years.

_____ **13.** Probing questions were asked by the lawyer for the defence.

_____ **14.** There are 60 officers on the local police service.

_____ **15.** Do not disturb the crime scene. (The subject _you_ is understood.)

_____ **16.** The dog picked up the scent of the missing child.

_____ **17.** After the robbery, did the first officer on the scene interview the bystanders?

__X__ **18.** The pedestrian was hit by the car at the corner of Sanford and Elgin. (This correction is a suggestion only.)

_____ **19.** The witness testified under oath.

_____ **20.** The victim was sent to the hospital for observation.

_____ **21.** Some officers dislike giving traffic tickets.

_____ **22.** There appeared to be no more witnesses to interview.

_____ **23.** Are you patrolling the east side of the city this shift?

_____ **24.** After investigating an occurrence, write your report as soon as possible. (The subject _you_ is understood.)

_____ **25.** Is his partner new in the department?

Exercise 7.2 Correcting Fragment Sentences

The following are some possible ways to correct the sentences. They are not the only suitable answers.

1. The woman **was** accused of abducting the child.

OR

The woman accused of abducting the child **testified that she was the child's grandmother and was babysitting.**

2. **The inexperienced officer** forgot to read the accused his rights.

OR

Because the officer forgot to read the accused his rights, **the charges were dropped.**

3. **The officer** pulled the speeding vehicle over and gave the driver a ticket.

4. After the neighbours complained at 2 a.m., the **constable was** sent to investigate the noise.

OR

The neighbours complained at 2 a.m., **and** the constable **patrolling the area** was sent to investigate the noise.

5. The officer's shotgun and ammunition **were** in the trunk of his cruiser, which was parked down the street.

6. The police officer's presentation on teenagers' abuse of alcohol **was** to the Block Parent group who had assembled in the auditorium.

7. When the police officer asked the witness to the assault what she saw, her reply was, "**The assailant g**rabbed hold of the **woman's** purse, punched **her** in the face, and attempted to run away with the purse in his hand. **Fortunately,** two bystanders tackled him and held him until you arrived."

8. **More w**omen **are** working in non-traditional occupations such as policing and security, which have often been thought of **as dangerous** jobs held only by men.

OR

Women working in non-traditional occupations such as policing and security **are now performing duties that** have often been thought of **as dangerous** jobs held only by men.

9. My appraisal of her progres**s is that she is o**ften absent, **she h**anded five assignments in late**, and she t**alks incessantly in class.

10. At 12 p.m. the officers received the **call to r**espond to a 911 at the corner of East Avenue and Ralph Street. They raced to the scen**e w**here they found a black male of medium build lying on the sidewalk. His chest **was** covered in blood from what appeared to be a stab wound just below the breastbone. They moved the onlookers back, and called for an ambulance and backup**, a**nd, while one checked the victim, the other questioned the bystanders. Three of the people identified the victim's assailant as a white female, 5'6" in height, with blond hair, wearing blue jeans and a blue jean jacket. Her escape route **was** along Ralph Street into the busy downtown**, where she d**isappeared into the crowd.

Exercise 7.3   Avoiding Run-On Sentences

The following are some possible ways to correct the sentences. They are not the only suitable answers.

____ 1. The city councillors supported community policing. **They** wanted kiosks set up in all the malls.

Because the city councillors supported community policing, they wanted kiosks set up in all the malls.

The city councillors supported community policing**; furthermore,** they wanted kiosks set up in all the malls.

____ 2. The officer directing traffic appeared to be very warm. **I** could see the perspiration running down her face.

The officer directing traffic appeared to be very warm, **since** I could see the perspiration running down her face.

The officer directing traffic appeared to be very warm; I could see the perspiration running down her face.

The officer directing traffic appeared to be very warm; **indeed**, I could see the perspiration running down her face.

_____ **3.** We completed our investigation of the robbery. **Then** another emergency called us across town.

After we completed our investigation of the robbery, another emergency called us across town.

We completed our investigation of the robbery; **moreover**, another emergency called us across town.

_X_ **4.** Last night I walked my beat for five hours without a break because there was a lot of dissension between the residents and the transients who refused to leave the neighbourhood.

_____ **5.** Three of the detectives watched from the observation van in case we needed assistance. **T**he rest of us infiltrated the underground organization to find the ring leader and those who protected him as they processed raw heroin, sold it on the street, **and laundered** their profits through the electrical business with which they were connected.

While three of the detectives watched from the observation van in case we needed assistance, the rest of us infiltrated the underground organization. **We were looking for** the ring leader and those who protected him as they processed raw heroin, sold it on the street, and then laundered their profits through the electrical business with which they were connected.

_____ **6.** There are many good police films made. **I** wish I could tell which show the officers' actual jobs and which glamourize the position.

Although there are many good police films made, I wish I could tell which show the officers' actual jobs and which glamourize the position.

There are many good police films made; **however**, I wish I could tell which show the officers' actual jobs and which glamourize the position.

_X_ **7.** John trained daily; he wanted to be accepted on the tactical squad.

_____ **8.** We questioned the child about his black eye and bruises. **H**is reply was hesitant.

When we questioned the child about his black eye and bruises, his reply was hesitant.

We questioned the child about his black eye and bruises; **however,** his reply was hesitant.

_____ 9. The RIDE officers pulled over 178 vehicles last night. **Thirteen** drivers had consumed alcohol over the legal limit.

Although the RIDE officers pulled over 178 vehicles last night, **only** 13 drivers had consumed alcohol over the legal limit.

The RIDE officers pulled over 178 vehicles last night**;** 13 drivers had consumed alcohol over the legal limit.

_____ 10. The community service officer visited four schools during the day. **T**hen he attended a home and school meeting that evening.

The community service officer visited four schools during the day, **and** then he attended a home and school meeting that evening.

The community service officer visited four schools during the day**; furthermore,** he attended a home and school meeting that evening.

_____ 11. The OPP may station their officers anywhere in Ontario. **S**ome officers may even be sent to Fort Albany.

Since the OPP may station their officers anywhere in Ontario, some officers may be sent to Fort Albany.

The OPP may station their officers anywhere in Ontario**; consequently,** some officers may even be sent to Fort Albany.

_____ 12. Many people at college tend to forget that a complete education involves both the body and the mind, and **students in most courses** don't take physical fitness seriously. **T**hose enrolled in the Police Foundations courses must realize how important it is that they be physically fit in order to secure a job once they graduate.

Many people at college tend to forget that a complete education involves both the body and the mind. **I**n most courses, students don't take physical fitness seriously, but those enrolled in the Police Foundations courses must realize how important it is that they be physically fit in order to secure a job once they graduate.

_____ 13. Police officers need to give objective reports. **T**hey must present the facts in an unbiased and unemotional way.

Police officers need to give objective reports, **so** they must present the facts in an unbiased and unemotional way.

Police officers need to give objective reports**; therefore,** they must present the facts in an unbiased and unemotional way.

____ **14.** At first the officers used shields and batons to protect themselves from the angry protesters. It was finally necessary for the officers to shoot tear gas into the crowd.

At first the officers used shields and batons to protect themselves from the angry protesters, **but** it was finally necessary for the officers to shoot tear gas into the crowd.

At first the officers used shields and batons to protect themselves from the angry protesters; **nevertheless**, it was finally necessary for the officers to shoot tear gas into the crowd.

____ **15.** Videotaped and CD-ROM instruction are now available for many subjects, including Police Foundations courses. Students may sit in front of a television or computer screen and observe lectures, read text, and perform exercises; however, problems sometimes arise when the students have questions the machines can't answer **and** there are no professors around to assist them. Another problem is that the machines can present the theory of, for example, interpersonal communication, without the students actually interacting with another human being. The students can't truly put what they have seen or read into practice and know whether or not their behaviour is acceptable and helpful. **Although** many feel that machines can easily replace the teacher, isn't the feedback received from others important to police officers, whose job it is not only to work with machines, but, more importantly, with the public?

THE COMMA

Exercise 7.4 Commas and Semicolons

1. Although the witness examined the photo lineup three times, he could not positively identify the suspect.

2. Constables Lee and Hussein were met at the accident by constables O'Hara, Perez, and Gauthier.

3. The suspect out-manoeuvred the police officer; however, he couldn't escape the police dog.

4. In most police service units, officers are expected to arrive early for all scheduled meetings.

5. The bystander said, "I didn't expect the police to respond so quickly."

6. The suspect was searched, handcuffed, and helped into the squad car.

7. When they arrived at the station, he was booked, photographed, fingerprinted, interrogated, and allowed to make a phone call.

8. His lawyer, who had bailed him out on several occasions, arrived shortly after the suspect was booked.

9. "I'm not sure, sir, if the fire department will be able to get your cat out of the tree," responded the desk sergeant.

10. Until he was promoted to detective, he was just like one of the guys.

11. Habib and Steve, both recent Police Foundations graduates, have been accepted on the local police service.

12. I wanted to apply for a job with the city police services, so I submitted my résumé, a cover letter, and letters of reference.

13. My credentials were good and my interview went well; consequently, my name was put on the hiring list.

14. Staff Sergeant Sung, the woman who interviewed me, assured me that I had a good chance of getting a job.

15. "A witness to the accident, Mr. John Henry," said the driver, "was standing on the corner."

16. To stay in shape for the fitness exam, she runs daily; furthermore, she works out in the gym three times a week, takes aerobics classes, and is active on the college swim team.

17. We searched the park, the beach, and the lakeshore for the missing little boy, yet we found no trace of him.

18. By running into the nearest store, the woman was able to escape her assailant.

19. Twice, he was late arriving for work. We know, therefore, that he will be put on report.

20. Five bystanders came forward, and each had a different description of the car.

THE APOSTROPHE

Exercise 7.5 Using Apostrophes To Show Possession

1. The victim's testimony was believed by the jurors. (*one victim*)

2. The ladies' purses were stolen while they swam.

3. Child care workers must inform the police about children's suspicious injuries.

4. Officers' in-car computers allow them to quickly check people's records.

5. The narcotics officer relies on his dog's nose to sniff out hidden drugs.

6. Twelve incident reports were recorded in the constable's notebook. *(one constable)*

7. In the late afternoon, the women's husbands returned from the weapons inspection. *(Here, "weapons inspection" is treated as one thing and not as an inspection of weapons.)*

8. The motorcycle gang's club house was raided by the tactical squad's senior officers.

9. The officer's demeanour indicated that she wanted the information right away.

10. When they reported the lone assailant's appearance, no bystander's description was the same as any other's.

11. If it had not been for the junkie's assistance, we would not have identified the suspects' car. *(one junkie; more than one suspect)*

12. The mountainous terrain made finding the man's wife and child difficult.

13. Tonight's weather may hinder our rescue efforts.

14. Her family's concern for her safety stems from her refusal to remove her guard dogs' muzzles.

15. Each security officer's job is to protect the celebrities during the Academy Awards presentations. *(Here, "Academy Awards presentations" is treated as one thing and not as presentations of Academy Awards.)*

16. The trial judge's influence on the jury members was evident.

17. Everybody's opinion of the jurors' verdict was different.

18. The criminal's hopes sank when he was refused early parole.

19. Some citizens' groups believe we should pay more attention to victims' rights than to criminals' liberty.

20. On my mother-in-law's advice, I applied to work in our police service's canine unit.

Exercise 7.6 Forming Contractions

1. The suspect **wouldn't** cooperate with the police.

2. **I've** found that too many people **don't** obey the rules of the road.

3. The officer said **she'd** requested assistance and **couldn't** proceed until more officers arrived.

4. **Who's** applied for a field placement with the local police service?

5. **They've** little concern for their dog's safety in most situations, but they **shouldn't** believe that nothing will ever happen.

6. **You're** the last person I expected to see drinking and driving!

7. The OPP **isn't** hiring right now; however, that **doesn't** mean it **won't** be looking for cadets in the new year.

8. **We've** had difficulty getting witnesses to come forward, and **I'm** concerned that **we'll** never be able to identify the hit and run driver.

9. There **aren't** many patrol cars in our neighbourhood because **they're** needed in other parts of the city.

10. The officer asked the children if **they'd** like to pet his police dog.

Exercise 7.7 Making Plural and Possessive Abbreviations

1. Officers from the OPP**'s** tactical squad requested information from the RCMP**'s** criminal investigation unit.

2. In elementary school we were told to learn our ABCs so that we could write without difficulty when we got older.

3. Some RCMPs worked with the CIA**'s** drug enforcement unit to break the cocaine ring.

4. Students in the Police Foundations Program are often referred to as PFPs.

5. Because they will work with the public, PFPs**'** communication skills must be good.

6. The Ontario PM**'s** office was swarmed by opposition MPs**'** secretaries, and the OPP was called in to escort them out.

7. After WWII, some RCAF officers flew supply missions for the OPP**'s** Northern Ontario Relief Organization.

8. Remember to dot all your i**'s** and cross all your t**'s**.

Exercise 7.8 Making Plural and Possessive Numbers

1. During the 1950s**'** housing boom, cities grew, and larger police departments were required.

2. The late 1980s**'** growth in town sizes was reminiscent of the growth of the 1950s.

3. I felt sorry for the traffic officer because the temperature today was in the high 30s, and with the humidity, it soared to the low 40s.

4. The average mark on the entrance exam was in the 80s, but the applicants knew that the year 2004**'s** requirements would dictate that they get in the 90s.

5. Before the '90s' switch to coin, our paper currency was in 1s, 2s, 5s, 10s, 20s, 50s, and so on; now we no longer have 1s and 2s.

Exercise 7.9 Making Nouns Ending in "S" Possessive

1. Sergeant Gibbins was a veteran investigator for the police service; therefore, when Gibbins's staff sergeant gave him traffic duty on a Paris side road, he knew something was wrong.

2. Three officers failed the inspection: Aramass's revolver was on the car seat beside him; Harness's notebook was not complete; and Thomas's reports had not been filed for two weeks.

3. The OPP graduation celebration was held at the Smith Falls' community centre.

4. Tess's check of the alarm system at the Monsamis' house was greatly appreciated by Mr. Monsami because he and his family were leaving on vacation and he wanted to make sure that the alarm was working properly.

5. The witness's statement was recorded in Constable Swiss's notebook.

6. When the Davises returned home after an evening out and found their front door open and lights on inside, they went to Ms Waters's house, next door, to phone the police.

PARALLEL STRUCTURE

Exercise 7.10 Parallel Structure Corrections

1. The recruit was a tall, handsome, muscular athlete.

2. Long lectures, difficult books, and frequent tests are part of every cadet's life.

3. She liked the sturdiness and road performance of the car.

4. His argument for free parking was clear, coherent, and passionate.

5. The officer will show you where to go and the turns to make on the way.

6. Experiencing job satisfaction is as important as earning money.

7. Pay careful attention to spelling, punctuation, and word usage in your reports.

8. The Willow Tree will have its alarm system installed on either Monday or Tuesday.

9. We left Burtch Correctional Facility at noon and arrived at Kingston Penitentiary at nine.

10. He wanted to take his stereo system, television, and Sega games with him to the Milton Correctional Facility.

11. The squeegee kid said he would neither stop interrupting nor leave the driver he had been harassing alone with the officer.

12. The elderly man went into great detail about his assailant's physical appearance and curious habit of pulling at his ear.

13. I believe the day will come when, to drive on highways, we will pay at toll booths or have a bill sent to our homes.

14. Mary excels in vehicle training, target practice, and self-defence.

15. In appearance she was untidy and over-dressed, and she wore too many jewels.

OR

In appearance she was untidy and over-dressed, and over-adorned with jewels.

16. The villagers gave José a perfect description of the two men and told him that the men had started north on foot a week before.

OR

The villagers told José that the men had started north on foot a week before, and gave him a perfect description of them.

17. I asked the security guards to patrol the beach, mingle in the crowds, and break up any disturbances.

18. If a car overturned and burned, men trapped inside could be rescued by passersby.

19. A recruit is expected to come to the examination clear-headed, well prepared, and determined to do her best.

20. Teamwork is displayed by a constable who respects his partner and his actions, and who defends him in difficult situations.

ELIMINATING WORDINESS AND INFLATED LANGUAGE

Exercise 7.11   Eliminating Wordiness 1

1. The stain on your shirt is **not visible** (or **invisible**).

2. The victim liked the officer **because** she was helpful.

3. The Toronto Police Service's uniform is **similar to** Hamilton's.

4. Your traffic ticket **is** $260.

5. **Because/Since** there was a robbery, the officers rushed to the scene.

6. The canine unit will arrive **later**.

7. **Until** the ambulance arrived, the constable performed CPR.

8. The officer repeated his instructions (**again**). *(if he repeated them once already)*

9. **Enclosed** is my application for employment with your department.

10. He was a cadet **for** six months.

11. **Please** answer a few questions.

12. **No doubt** you've heard the news about the drug bust.

13. The suspect said to the constable, "I don't have an answer **now**."

14. **If** the GATB test is fair, I'll do well.

15. I'm writing **concerning** your request for a community home safety presentation.

Exercise 7.12 Eliminating Wordiness 2

1. During the chase, the suspects drove their car into a pond. **Then** their car stalled, and the suspects ran into the woods.

2. **He** strives to stay in touch with the public.

   OR

   That officer strives to stay in touch with the public.

3. **An honest person** is usually not arrested.

4. **Some people** would rather rob a bank than work for minimum wage.

5. When I arrived at the crime scene, **she was there**.

6. **I don't think** the witness has told us all she knows.

7. **My sergeant** is always helpful.

8. When we arrived at the gang fight, we were **surrounded**.

9. The constable received a **gift** from his sergeant.

10. The suspect's hair is **long**; in fact, it hangs past his shoulders.

11. The officer asked the judge if he could **refer** to his notebook to refresh his memory.

12. The constable said to the victim, "Would you please **repeat** what you said."

13. There were **two kinds** of weapons used in the robbery.

14. The cadets received a **complimentary copy** of the *Highway Traffic Act*.

15. **During the winter** officers may be chilled to the bone while on traffic duty.

16. The **unique** vase has been missing since the robbery.

17. The police informant's **past** warned the sergeant not to trust her.

OR

The police informant's **history** warned the sergeant not to trust her.

18. The **result** of the investigation was that a suspect was arrested.

19. When we wrote the GATB test, we took pens, pencils, paper, **et cetera** with us.

20. The thugs' **custom** was to don balaclavas before invading people's homes.

Exercise 7.13   Eliminating Wordiness and Avoiding Inflated Language

The officer walked toward the automobile. The driver rolled the window down and looked at the officer, asking, "Why have you pulled me over?"

The officer asked, "Do you know, ma'am, how you were driving on the highway?"

She replied, "Why, officer, I am amazed that you stopped my car to question my driving. My driving is harmless!"

The officer replied, "Ma'am, you displayed little concern for other drivers on the road. You were driving carelessly. Therefore, I am giving you a ticket, which you may pay, or you may appear in court."

SUBJECT–VERB AGREEMENT

Exercise 7.14   Subjects Not in Prepositional Phrases

1. My sergeant, as well as my partner, **has** accompanied me on patrol.

2. Although many people witnessed the accident, only one of the 12 **was** able to give me a detailed description of what happened.

3. My family and home life, not to mention my recreational time, **suffer** when I work the night shift.

4. The desk sergeant, along with those in mobile units, **needs** to understand computer fundamentals.

5. All our duties, including report writing, **are** important.

6. An officer who walks the beat, as well as those who patrol the suburbs in cars, **records** daily occurrences in a notebook.

7. A detective and a forensic officer **were** present at the scene.

8. My spouse, as well as my superiors, **wants** me to apply for the canine unit.

9. The repeat offender, in accordance with the advice of his counsellors, **has** enrolled in an anger management program.

10. The 12 jurors, one of whom believes in the accused's innocence, **remain** locked in deliberation.

Exercise 7.15 Verbs Coming Before Subjects

1. When **do** you meet with the Block Parent group?

2. In the middle of the field **stand** the memorials to officers killed in the line of duty.

3. There **is** an unsigned report on the sergeant's desk.

4. Which **was** the bystander's statement recorded by you?

5. Over the fence **scramble** the suspects, with the police right behind them.

6. Of all the women in the lineup, which **appears** to be the one you saw running away from the burning building?

7. Whom **has** the RCMP investigated concerning the stock fraud? (*Here, the RCMP acts as a group and is therefore a collective noun, making it singular.*)

8. There **are** many reasons why the RIDE program should remain in effect.

9. In the trunk of the patrol car **are** the officers' shotguns.

10. **Does** the witness have any further information?

Exercise 7.16 Agreement of Indefinite Pronouns and Verbs

1. Each of the suspects **has** red hair.

2. There **is** someone patrolling this part of the city every evening.

3. Everything we know about the sniper, including his last known address, **has** been published in the newspaper.

4. Nobody **seems** concerned about the break-and-enters during the Christmas season.

5. The 911 caller said, "Someone **needs** to send a fire truck. One of my cats **was** chased up a tree, and it can't get down."

Exercise 7.17 Agreement of Compound Subjects and Verbs

1. Both the officers and the suspect **were** covered in mud after running through the swamp.

2. Neither the victim nor his assailants **are** willing to tell us what started the fight.

3. I don't know if either the Block Parent groups or the Street Proofing Association **receives** community funding.

4. The security officers or the head of mall security **goes** to high schools and **talks** to students about the penalties for shoplifting.

5. Not only American cigarettes, but also contraband liquor, **has** been smuggled across the border into Canada.

6. The tracking dog and its handler **were** commended for finding the lost child.

7. Either the complainant or the accused **is** lying.

8. Not only the counsel for the defence, but also the defendants, **seem** nervous about the outcome of the trial.

9. Constable Perez or others from her unit **ride** through the park every day.

10. At night, children and adults alike **are** at risk in certain parts of the city.

FAULTY MODIFIERS

Exercise 7.18 Misplaced Modifiers

1. **The** young constable attended a party for the chief of police, who was retiring **at the age of 65**.

2. The suspect, **who was from Thunder Bay,** was running along an alley. *(Note the change in wording here.)*

3. **From our window,** we saw the car strike the telephone pole.

4. **With his partner,** the officer drove the patrol car down the city street that had not been plowed.

5. The informant **often** gives us information.

6. The detective *carefully* approached the suspect's house. *(Note the change in wording here.)*

7. When the woman accused her boyfriend of infidelity, she could **hardly** contain her anger.

8. The thieves *who* **broke in through the window** stole all her stereo equipment. *(Note the change in wording here.)*

9. The newspaper photographer showed **the police officer the robbery pictures** that he had shot.

10. Community policing involves being visible as a helping part of the community and not **merely** *being seen* as law enforcers.

   OR

   Community policing involves being visible as a helping part of the community and not **only** *being seen* as law enforcers.

11. My sergeant told me they **badly** needed someone who could translate Cantonese.

12. She bought a coffee **that cost $1.25** for her partner, and he drank **almost** the whole thing in one gulp.

13. The dog searched for the missing child, ***who was* wearing a blue coat and running shoes**. *(Note the change in wording here.)*

14. The Crown attorney had **just** left when the jurors returned with their verdict.

15. Parole officers should be aware of the location and activities of their clients, **so that they are deterred from becoming repeat offenders.**

16. The undercover narcotics officer described the smuggler as a tall, white, *gray-haired* American in a fancy boat. *(Note the change in wording here.)*

17. The police service serves **nearly** two million people in this area.

18. **In the middle of her shift**, Constable Longboat responded to a public disturbance call.

19. The accident, ***which occurred in blinding snow on an icy road***, involved three cars. *(Note the change in wording here.)*

20. The surveillance crew, **in their unmarked van**, watched the drug dealer sell cocaine to school children.

Exercise 7.19   Dangling Modifiers

The following answers may differ from your answers since there are many ways to correct the sentences.

1. **While I was** training for the fitness exam, a universal weight fell and narrowly missed my knee.

2. While **we were** driving to the scene of an accident, the dispatcher gave us the details.

3. **While walking down the hall,** the public service officers found the Block Parent meeting room.

4. After arresting a suspect, **you should read him or her** the rights to counsel from the *Charter of Rights and Freedoms*.

5. We answered the B & E call, but, upon entering the building, **we found no one.**

6. Before leaving after your shift, **you should complete your reports** in full.

7. **While the officer was s**peaking to a public school about street proofing, a grade 5 boy asked about bullying.

8. While **I was** driving through an intersection on a green light, a blue Chevrolet ran the red and hit my car on the passenger side.

9. **After *the cross-border shopper paid* almost $250 for his purchases,** most of ***his* new goods** were confiscated **when he crossed** the border. (*Note the change in wording here.*)

10. After **the inmates rioted** in the prison, the guards locked **them** in their cells.

11. **When we were p**ursuing the speeding car, **we** turned on **the siren.**

12. Determined to catch the Mafia boss, **we started** a surveillance.

13. Unobservant drivers are a hazard **for a** traffic officer.

14. In an attempt to relate to community youth, **the officers planned** a basketball game.

15. While **I was** on duty last night, it rained.

16. The jurors found **the man on trial for manslaughter** guilty.

17. After watching the woman empty her ashtray on the roadside, **the officer gave her** a ticket for littering.

18. Since the accused broke the conditions of his bail, **he was arrested.**

19. **The report of** vandalism in progress **proved** the Neighbourhood Watch program **was** invaluable.

20. ***The officer locked*** the shotgun in the trunk of the patrol car ***so that it would be*** out of sight of any bystanders. (*Note the change in wording here.*)

THE PAST TENSE

Exercise 7.20   Simple Past Tense

At 10 p.m., P.C. Lee and P.C. Roanski **received** a 911, possible stabbing, call at 123 Howard Street. When the officers **arrived**, P.C. Lee and P.C. Roanski **found** the victim on the pavement in a pool of blood, with what **appeared** to be a stab wound in his left side. The ambulance **was** already there, and the attendants **said** they **wanted** P.C. Lee and P.C. Roanski's OK to move him. A group of inquisitive bystanders **watched** as P.C. Lee **secured** the area and P.C. Roanski **asked** for information.

Only one onlooker **said** he **had** information. He **saw** the victim and another person as they **came** out of the bar across the street. Their loud voices **caught** his attention as they **argued**. Then the victim **shoved** the other person, and, after another loud exchange and more aggressive pushing, the victim **fell** to the ground. The other person **stared** at the victim for what **seemed** like a minute, and then **ran** east down Howard Street toward downtown.

Exercise 7.21 Past Progressive and Simple Past Tenses

As a woman **was crossing** the border from the United States into Canada, she **stopped** at the Customs booth. The Customs officer **asked** her citizenship. When she **replied** that she **was** American, the Customs officer **asked** her where she **was** from, what her destination **was**, and how long she **intended** to be in Canada. She **said** she **was** from Chicago and that she **was going** to meet her elderly relatives who **were moving** to Owen Sound in a couple of days. She **wanted** to arrive there before them as a surprise, and to stay with them for a week or two to help them unpack.

While the woman **was speaking**, the Customs officer **was looking** in her car. All of her possessions **seemed** to be in the interior. To him, it **looked** as though the woman **was planning** to spend longer than a couple of weeks in Canada, and something **was**n't right with her story. He **asked** her to wait for a moment and **referred** to his notes.

While he **was checking** the most recent bulletins, the woman **sped** off. Then he **knew** for sure something **was** wrong. The Customs officer immediately **called** for assistance, and the police **were pursuing** her within minutes.

He **was** wise to ask for assistance. The woman **was** a wanted felon and **was**n't **intending** to visit anyone. She **was** simply **planning** to hide in Canada. Also, she **was carrying** a loaded revolver, which she **had used** to rob a convenience store the night before. The police **told** him that the woman **confessed** that she **was going** to threaten him with the gun if he **questioned** her further.

Exercise 7.22 Past Perfect, Past Progressive, and Simple Past Tenses

The jail guard **had seen** the inmates angry before, but never **had** he **experienced** anything like this. They **were yelling** and **throwing** things against the bars of their cells. It **was frightening** for the young guard because he **had heard** that this **was** the first sign of a prison uprising.

He **made** sure he **had** securely **locked** his cell block and **went** to his supervisor's office. There he **reported** what the inmates **were doing** to their living quarters. The supervisor **asked** if he **knew** what **had caused** the problem and if he **had tried** to calm the men under his care. The guard **thought** he **had heard** one man threaten another, but that **was** not unusual. Then he

remembered that he and some other guards **had broken** up a vicious fight earlier that day. It **concerned** the turf of two antagonistic groups. That, he realized, **had caused** the near-riot in his cell block.

Exercise 7.23   Using All Four Verb Tenses

From their van, the surveillance team **had been watching** the house for hours and **had seen** nothing. They **had** even **been considering** quitting for the day and one officer **was getting** ready to pack his equipment away. Suddenly, the man **walked** out of his house. The team in the van **hadn't expected** this, so they **had** to scramble to get ready.

The man **was carrying** a pail and a car wash brush and **was tugging** on a hose as he **approached** his car, which he **was** obviously **preparing** to wash. For an hour, the surveillance team **photographed** his every move as he **filled** the pail, **bent** over and **dipped** the brush in the sudsy water, and **proceeded** to scrub his car. They **had been waiting** for an opportunity like this to catch him in the act.

When they **had taken** enough pictures, the team leader, wearing a wire, **left** the van and **approached** the man. She **asked** him if washing his car **was relaxing** for him, and he eagerly **responded** in the affirmative. Then she **asked** if he **had noticed** that his muffler **was dangling**. He **said** he **knew**, and that he **had** just **been planning** to repair it himself but **wanted** the driveway to dry first. He even **leaned** under the car to point out the damaged area.

Now the team leader **knew** she **had** enough evidence. The surveillance team **had photographed** the man's every move, and they **had taped** her conversation with him. As she **walked** away, a sly smile **was** even **beginning** to cross her face. The man they **had been watching** can now be charged with insurance fraud. His severe back injury **wasn't** as debilitating as he **had been claiming**.

USING CAPITAL LETTERS

Exercise 7.24   Using Capitals Correctly

1. <u>S</u>ometimes it is impossible to tell the criminal from the victim.

2. <u>T</u>he young offender was attending <u>A</u>ncaster <u>H</u>igh and <u>V</u>ocational <u>S</u>chool when he was arrested by <u>O</u>fficer <u>C</u>hen for drug trafficking.

3. <u>T</u>he young constable's grandmother always had confidence in his ability to succeed as a law enforcement officer.

4. <u>S</u>o that he could attend the <u>H</u>anukkah celebrations in <u>K</u>ingston with his family, <u>C</u>onstable <u>B</u>romberg asked for vacation time in <u>D</u>ecember.

5. <u>T</u>he best narcotics sniffer in the canine unit is <u>S</u>top <u>G</u>ap, the <u>G</u>erman shepherd handled by <u>S</u>ergeant <u>P</u>erez.

6. **M**any **C**hinese-, **I**ndian-, and **S**panish-speaking people are now applying for law enforcement positions in this area.

7. **W**hen the **p**resident of the **U**nited **S**tates recently visited **C**anada, the **RCMP** was on full alert.

8. **T**he book entitled **A** **R**eport **W**riting **G**uide for the **L**aw **E**nforcement **P**rofession will soon be a mandatory resource for all officers.

9. **T**he officer asked, "**W**ere you able to see your assailant, **M**r. **W**ilke?"

   "**I**t was impossible for me to see who attacked me," the victim replied, " because **I** was jumped from behind."

   "**D**o you remember, when he demanded your wallet, if he had an accent?" asked the officer.

   "**I**t sounded **S**cottish, **W**elsh, or **I**rish, or something like that. **I** know it wasn't a **N**orwegian accent," answered the victim.

10. **W**e tracked the suspect as she drove south to **L**ake **O**ntario and then took the 401 east toward the **E**astern **T**ownships of **Q**uebec.

EDITING

Exercise 7.25   A Grammar and Spelling Review

The **RCMP's** Officer LeDuc **has been** talked about since her vacation last summer. She rented a cabin in the **northern** part of the province, near Moose River, for a vacation. She wanted to get away from the busy city and just relax, but what began as a quiet holiday soon became more exciting than she had wished.

After a few days at the cabin, Officer LeDuc drove into town to look around. She stopped at a variety store for some chocolate bars, and, as she was leaving the parking lot, she **saw** three people, **wearing balaclavas and carrying shotguns and bulky sacks,** run out of the local bank. They jumped into a black Ford van and sped off as people ran out of the bank yelling that they'**d** been robbed and pointing in the direction the van had gone.

She phoned the local **police service** from her car, but their nearest patrol car was 50 kilometres away. Because she was off duty an**d,** there-fore, unequipped to handle the situation, her only choice was to follow the **fugitives** until the local police could catch up.

Officer LeDuc stayed well back from the van, and the **occupants** didn't seem to notice she was following them. They followed the high-way **south** about 15 kilometres. **T**hen they turned onto Little Point Road, a narrow, **dirt, s**ide road, posted with a "Boat Launch" sign. This worried Officer LeDuc, since she **wasn't** sure of the territory **a**nd knew she was outnumbered. However, **s**he also knew the road led to the water, a perfect escape route for the **robbery** suspect**s. A**s she turned down the road after them, she was glad she'**d** stayed in constant touch with the local **dispatcher**.

Knowing she had no time to waste, Officer LeDuc sped down the dirt roa**d, u**p hill**s, a**nd around sharp bends, until she could see the dust created by the van in front of her. Soon she realized she was righ**t. A**t the end of the road, a boat was docked at the **east** side of a pier. The boat was untie**d, t**he motor was running, **a**nd the driver, **w**ho saw Officer **LeDuc's** car racing toward the**m, motioned** to the people in the van to hurry.

Officer LeDuc was close enough to see that the three suspects, now without their balaclava**s,** were me**n, b**ut she couldn't get to the pier fast enough to prevent them from getting into the boat. She could tel**l, though,** that they **had left** the van in such haste that they had only taken the sack**s** and **had left** all their **paraphernalia** in the van. Although she was a distance away, she must have frightened the suspects as she leapt from her car because, to get away, the driver gunned the motor, **a**nd it stalled.

The driver **tried** to restart the motor, but to no avail. **Officer LeDuc** could hear, **in the distance,** the approaching sirens of the local police. Knowing she had to do something to stop the suspects, she **seized** a chocolate bar from her car seat. Using her door as a shield, she pointed **the chocolate bar** at the suspect**s,** identified herself as a **p**olice **o**fficer, and ordered them to put their hands in the air. To her surprise, **t**hey complied. She was able to **detain** them until her backup **arrived,** and they took the men into custody.

From that day forward, Officer LeDuc **has been** known as the candy bar **c**onstabl**e** for **her unique** arrest.